Participant Manual

for use with

Merlin
A Marketing Simulation

Philip H. Anderson

David A. Beveridge

Leigh Lawton

Timothy W. Scott

McGraw Hill Irwin

Boston   Burr Ridge, IL   Dubuque, IA   Madison, WI   New York   San Francisco   St. Louis
Bangkok   Bogotá   Caracas   Kuala Lumpur   Lisbon   London   Madrid   Mexico City
Milan   Montreal   New Delhi   Santiago   Seoul   Singapore   Sydney   Taipei   Toronto

Irwin

Participant Manual for use with
MERLIN: A MARKETING SIMULATION
Philip H. Anderson, David A. Beveridge, Leigh Lawton and Timothy W. Scott

Published by McGraw-Hill/Irwin, an imprint of The McGraw-Hill Companies, Inc., 1221 Avenue of the Americas, New York, NY 10020. Copyright © 2004
by the McGraw-Hill Companies, Inc. All rights reserved.

1 2 3 4 5 6 7 8 9 0 QPD/QPD 0 9 8 7 6 5 4 3

ISBN 0-07-288775-3

www.mhhe.com

The McGraw Hill Companies

Table of Contents:

iv

A List of Exhibits:

CHAPTER 1

OVERVIEW

WHAT IS *MERLIN: A MARKETING SIMULATION?*

Merlin: A Marketing Simulation is a computer-based model that simulates the marketing management operations of a small company. You or your team will make the decisions necessary to run that company. Chapter 4 describes your company and the products it sells. We designed *Merlin* to help you improve your skills in managing the marketing operations of an enterprise. The simulation will also allow you to demonstrate your understanding of marketing concepts in a competitive, but safe environment. Working with this simulation is challenging, but manageable. We hope it will bring to life the topics you study in your marketing classes or read about in a marketing textbook, so that you can better see and understand the issues involved in formulating and implementing a marketing strategy. The chance to test your ideas is one of the best ways to learn about the field of marketing. Marketing managers are inherently action oriented. *Merlin* provides you with the opportunity to put what you have learned into action.

There actually are two versions of *Merlin*: *Merlin – Solo* and *Merlin – Team*. In *Merlin – Team*, you manage a company that competes against other companies run by students in your class. Each student-run company operates in the same marketplace and competes directly with other student-run companies. In *Merlin – Team*, the administrator uses the computer to process decisions that students make regarding the operation of their companies after collecting decisions from all participants.

Merlin – Solo is a play-alone version of *Merlin: A Marketing Simulation*. Rather than vying with other student-run companies, you compete against semi-intelligent companies managed by the computer. While these computer-run companies act rationally, they are not all-knowing, perfect competitors.

Your assignment is to manage the operations of your company, acting as the marketing executive responsible for making decisions about the marketing aspects of the business. The decisions you make will include financing the costs of the marketing and production operations, and the purchase of competitive information. Practicing with *Merlin – Team* or *Merlin – Solo* will sharpen your managerial skills.

You will compete with other companies selling similar products in your industry's marketplace. The computer will process your decisions and those of the other companies and provide reports regarding how well each company performed. The *Merlin* software uses the decisions you and your competitors make to determine how many units each company sells during a three-month period (i.e., quarter) and to provide operations, marketing, and financial reports for your company. You will manage your company for several quarters, analyzing the results of each quarter to help you make decisions for the next quarter's operations. What follows is a discussion of how the *Merlin* simulation works.

HOW THE *MERLIN* SIMULATION WORKS

The *Merlin* program contains mathematical formulas and sets of rules. These formulas and rules allow the program to simulate, or imitate, the results that a business decision would have in the real world. So, for example, the *Merlin* program can determine how a company's sales would be affected by the price that it sets for its product when compared with the prices of its competitors' products.

You will make decisions regarding the marketing of two products in three sales territories for each period of operation that you manage your *Merlin* company. Each period of operation represents one quarter (i.e., three months) of a calendar year. You begin managing *Merlin* operations in Quarter 1 (January – March) and can continue to make decisions through succeeding quarters. Just as you would if you were managing an actual business enterprise, your goal is to manage your *Merlin* company as efficiently and effectively as possible. As you progress through each quarter of operation, you should work to improve your performance by analyzing your results, identifying your mistakes, and modifying your decisions to eliminate those mistakes.

MERLIN'S THREE STAGES IN A DECISION-ROUND

There are three stages involved in working with the *Merlin* simulation. They are (1) the Forecasting Stage, (2) the Processing Stage, and (3) the Results Stage. In the Forecasting Stage, you enter decisions to test "what if" assumptions and then modify those decisions until you enter a set of decisions you think are the best. In the Processing Stage, the program assesses the decisions of all competitors to determine market share allocations for each company and the consequent profitability of each company. (In *Merlin – Team*, other student-run teams supply competitors' decisions while in *Merlin – Solo* the computer generates competitors' decisions.) In the Results Stage you respond to the results of the processing of your decisions, looking at your company's reports to assess your actual performance versus what you forecasted it to be during the Forecasting Stage. You then use your analysis in a new Forecasting Stage as you begin the next decision round.

The Forecasting Stage

In the Forecasting Stage, you will make decisions regarding (a) marketing (e.g., pricing, promotion, and quality of your products), (b) manufacturing (e.g., how many units of your products to order from a sub-contractor), and (c) financing (e.g., requesting a loan to pay current bills). Once you have entered your decisions, you can look at *forecasted* reports for your company based on the decisions you just entered. You can view these *forecasted* reports using the Reports option on the Menu bar. (We explain how to do this in Chapter 3.) After analyzing these reports, you can enter new decisions to try to improve your *forecasted* results. Entering new decisions will allow you to test "what-if" assumptions and then to modify those decisions until you find the set of decisions you think are the best. You can enter new decisions as often as you like before you choose to process your entries. There is no limit to the number of times you can enter new decisions. The last set of decisions that you enter and save will be used in the Processing Stage.

The Processing Stage

Once you are satisfied with the decisions you have entered, your decisions must be processed before you can move to the next quarter of operation (e.g., from Quarter 1 to Quarter 2). In *Merlin – Solo*, you simply instruct the computer to do this by selecting the "Process Industry" option under File on the Menu bar. Processing the industry commits you to the last set of decisions you entered. This means that once you process your decisions for a quarter, you cannot alter your decisions or the results for that quarter. Your next set of decisions will be for the next quarter of operation and will be based on the results of the quarter of operation you just completed. For example, once you process your Quarter 1 decisions, your next set of decisions will be for Quarter 2 regardless of how much you would like to change what you did in Quarter 1.

The processing stage of the *Team* version of *Merlin* is handled very differently from the *Solo* version. In the team version of *Merlin*, your decisions must be evaluated against other student-run companies. Consequently, you and all of your competitors must submit your decisions to the administrator for processing. The administrator can process the decisions for a quarter *only* after he or she has collected the decisions for *all* competitors. If the decisions for even one company are missing, the simulation cannot proceed. Once the simulation administrator has processed the decisions for a quarter they cannot be altered. Your administrator will return the results of your decisions and you will be ready to move on to the next quarter's operations.

Having to live with the decisions you have made is a part of organizational life. For example, the marketing team for Wal-Mart may use a model to test the effect of varying pricing strategies (e.g., higher price, but fewer unit sales) on profitability for the company. They will likely test many variations to the price versus sales trade-off. However, once they make the decision on the price of a product and the advertisement has run in the local newspaper, it is impossible to change the price (and the consequent sales results) for that advertisement. All Wal-Mart can do is to make a pricing change in *next* week's newspaper ad. So, once you choose to implement your decisions (i.e., process the quarter), you will also have to live with the consequences of those decisions for that quarter and make adjustments in your decisions for subsequent quarters.

In *Merlin – Solo* your competition consists of 11 computer-managed companies operating in the marketplace. While the computer competitors behave act rationally we designed *Merlin – Solo* so that you can establish a competitive advantage in the industry. When working with *Merlin – Solo* you will always manage Company #1. In *Merlin – Team*, the number of teams in your industry will be determined by the simulation administrator and will depend upon the number of student participants. Your administrator will let you know which company you're managing (Company #1 or Company #2, etc.)

Having the computer manage the companies you compete with in *Merlin – Solo* simplifies the procedure for processing your decisions. In *Merlin – Solo* the computer makes the decisions for the competing companies. Consequently, whenever you have completed your decisions for your company, you can process the decisions yourself for all the companies in the industry. *Merlin – Solo* eliminates the need for an administrator to collect and process the decisions of the companies operating in an industry. This allows you to play the game by yourself, at your own pace, not tied to anyone else's schedule. *Merlin – Solo* allows you to work with the software without having to wait for decisions from the competing companies, nor wait for an administrator to process company decisions. In addition, if you perform poorly against the computer competitors, you can stop playing the current setup and start a new competition quickly and easily (discussed below).

The Results Stage

Once your decisions have been processed, the *Merlin* program will generate reports that show how well your company performed in competition with the other companies in your industry. The program will determine how many sales each company made based on their marketing efforts relative to the competition and will provide individual marketing, operations, and financial reports for each company. In *Merlin – Team*, your administrator will return a disk or a file to you that will enable you to view your results. With *Merlin – Solo* you can access your results immediately after you have processed your decisions.

You will use the results of the quarter just processed as the basis for your decisions for the next quarter of operation. For example, maybe in Quarter 1 your price for Product 1 was too high compared to your competitors. If this resulted in an increase of inventory for that product, your Quarter 2 operations will reflect the cost of carrying that extra inventory. It would be up to you to adjust your pricing of Product 1 in Quarter 2 to avoid repeating the problem in Quarter 3. In other words, you will use your analysis of the results of a quarter that was just processed to guide you as you make your adjustments in your decisions and forecasts for the next quarter of operations. So once you have processed a quarter and analyzed the results, you will return to the Forecasting Stage and repeat the three-stage sequence.

HOW TO APPROACH THE SIMULATION

Managing a business is a blend of art and science. This means the process of managing requires working with both the facts of the situation you are facing and with your intuition regarding how to succeed in that environment. Emphasizing one of these at the expense of the other makes you a less effective manager. Intuitive problem-solvers make decisions without considering all of the data available to them. They are more concerned with their "gut feelings" than with the realities they face. Ignoring these realities results in decisions that are ineffective in resolving problems. By contrast, problem-solvers who rely completely on facts tend not to consider the aspects of a problem that cannot be easily reduced to numbers. Certainly you cannot quantify everything that contributes to the resolution of a problem. This approach, then, also leaves out key components of a problem's solution. *Merlin* will give you a chance to develop and practice both kinds of managerial thinking. Although you must work with the detail of the numbers generated in your *Merlin* reports, you must also get a feel for the total simulated business environment created by *Merlin*. Learning to manage both of these dimensions of a problem will make you a more effective marketing manager, not only of your *Merlin* company, but also in your subsequent business experiences.

Merlin – Team and *Merlin – Solo* can be played alone or your instructor may choose to have you manage your company as part of a group. Many college participants dislike working in a group. They feel that it is not like work in "the real world." In fact, groups working with a *Merlin* company face almost exactly the same problems that a work group in any business organization has to face. Managers in a business organization do much of their work in teams. Working with a group of individuals requires learning how to manage competing ideas and egos while successfully accomplishing the group's goal. This is a common experience in modern organizations. It is also a necessary element in successfully managing the *Merlin* simulation. In business, as in the *Merlin* simulation, each participant's knowledge, motivation, determination, and time available, affects the success of the enterprise. Learning to work together cooperatively is a critical ingredient for success in any business enterprise. One of the keys for anyone to be successful in an enterprise is to learn how to use the talents of others. Managers that try to do it all by themselves, limit the growth and success of their business.

Backup Your Company Disk. We encourage you to make copies of your *Merlin* company disk. You should keep a backup copy in case the original disk is lost, damaged, or destroyed. We ***strongly recommend*** that you make a backup copy of your disk after every time you exit the program. The information stored on your disk is important.

PURPOSES OF *MERLIN*

Working with *Merlin* will help you to:
- Experience problems and issues involved in managing a marketing-driven enterprise.
- Understand the importance of a marketing plan in guiding marketing decisions, including;
  - The importance of developing a common vision and coordinating the various elements of a product strategy, and
  - The need for planning as you make tactical moves to react to changing conditions,
- Acquire experiences to aid your comprehension of issues presented in marketing courses,
- Understand the relationships between marketing, operations, and finance,
- Understand the relationships between financial statements such as the cash flow statement, the income statement, and the balance sheet, and their tie to the marketing reports,
- Experience the dynamics of marketing against constantly changing competitor positions and the need for market research.

TIPS ON SUCCEEDING WITH *MERLIN*

The following are some tips to help you when you are working with the *Merlin* simulation:

- <u>Manage your time efficiently</u>. Learning how to manage time is a primary concern for any manager. It affects success in any business. There will never be enough time to do all that you would wish to do. Determine what issues to focus on (set priorities). Staying focused on these issues (efficiency) will have a significant impact on the effectiveness of the decisions you make. Working with *Merlin* gives you practice at managing this critical resource. Developing good time-management skills will increase your chances of success in your business career.

- <u>Manage your business; do not guess at your decisions</u>. You can either manage your company or guess when making decisions regarding the future. Managing the business involves having company goals, plus plans and strategies for meeting those goals. Use these goals, plans, and strategies to guide your decision-making. Guessing leads to making decisions randomly and without any consistency over time. This may be easier and more fun in the short run. You may even initially get better results than your competition. However, in the long run, if you make your decisions by guessing, you will not be able to outperform your competition. This is because you will not understand what you did that was correct and what you need to change to improve your position in subsequent quarters. Nor will you be sensitive to changes that your competitors are making or to changes in your economic environment. *Merlin* is the kind of project where effort is rewarded.

- <u>Learn from your failures as well as your successes</u>. Managers must always deal with their own and others' mistakes. When your decisions in *Merlin* do not give you the results you planned for, or they are not satisfactory for the long-term success of your company, analyze the results to see what you should do differently next time. A successful manager learns how to capitalize on success, recover from mistakes, and move forward to improve the company's position. You often can learn more from what you do wrong than from what you do right.

- <u>Do not worry if you are confused at first</u>. Participants are often confused when they begin working with the *Merlin* program. Remember, this is most likely a new form of learning experience for you. Working with a simulation requires *applying* your knowledge and skills to a business operation rather than *listening* to a lecture about the knowledge and skills needed to operate the business. It is a fundamental change to move from hearing to doing.

As with any new experience, it can be confusing and a bit overwhelming at first. However, after you make two or three sets of decisions, you should feel familiar with the rules of *Merlin* and become more comfortable with learning through active application rather than passive listening. Your willingness to invest the effort to learn your new environment will have a significant impact on your ability to outperform your competitors.

This exercise also replicates what you will experience in the world of business. Managers face a constantly changing business environment. Their ability to understand quickly new business situations significantly affects their personal and organizational success. You have only to think about the changes in computer technology you have witnessed over the past few years to recognize the importance of being able to adjust to changes around you.

HOW TO USE THIS MANUAL

Read this manual thoroughly, but do not try to memorize it. Instead, read the manual to get a sense of the business environment created by the simulation. Then, as you work on *Merlin*, refer to the appropriate sections of the manual for specific information. You will notice that the simulation's program contains much of the information supplied by this manual. For example, you can view the costs of operating the business through the Menu bar in the program. We will explain how to do this later in this manual.

When you get to Chapter 3, you will want to begin using the *Merlin* disk on your computer. Learning how to use the disk and keyboard to enter and record your decisions will make the rest of the manual easier to understand.

The appendixes have a number of forms and exhibits to help you manage your company. Look at them as you read the manual and refer to them later when you need the information.

The rest of the contents of this manual is outlined below.
- Chapter 2 instructs you on how to load the *Merlin* program onto your computer and to register the software so that it is operational.
- Chapter 3 introduces you to the simulation model created by the *Merlin* program. It gives you a quick guided tour of the simulation. We explain how to access current cost information through the Menu bar in the *Merlin* program in this chapter.
- Chapter 4 describes the company you will manage and the business environment in which you will operate.
- Chapter 5 reviews the fundamentals of marketing and shows how this simulation reflects these fundamentals.
- Chapter 6 discusses the decisions you will make and tells you how to enter them on the computer and onto your company disk.
- Chapter 7 describes the reports you will receive after each team makes decisions for each quarter of operation and after the computer has processed those decisions.

CHAPTER 2

LOADING AND REGISTERING THE *MERLIN* SOFTWARE

INTRODUCTION

In this chapter we will specify the computer requirements for using *Merlin*. We will also tell you how to load the *Merlin* software onto your computer's hard drive and how to register the software. The software consists of *Merlin* program files and certain Windows setup files. Once you have loaded these files onto a computer, you will not have to reload them on that particular computer. After loading *Merlin*, you must register the software before it will operate. You are permitted to register the software only one time (and for one computer). If you wish to use *Merlin* on more than one computer, you must purchase additional copies of the software.

INSTALLATION REQUIREMENTS

In order to install the *Merlin* programs on a computer, you will need a computer with a Microsoft Windows operating system. The *Merlin* programs do not work on computers that use the Apple operating system. You must also have an Internet connection and a valid key access number to register the software. This number is located with the CD at the back of this manual. We discuss each of these installation requirements below.

Equipment Needed

In order to operate the *Merlin – Team* and *Merlin – Solo* programs, you must have access to a personal computer system with the following characteristics:
- Windows 95, 98, 2000, ME, NT or Windows XP.
- 3 Megs of space on your hard disk.
- At least 1 disk drive.

Although optional, we advise that you use a printer so that you can generate printouts of your quarterly results. We also strongly recommend that you have a blank disk suitable for use with the PC to use to make backup copies of your *Merlin – Solo* files.

Internet Connection

To work with the *Merlin* programs, you will first have to register the programs. To register the programs, you will need to be connected to the Internet. If you do not have an internet connection, you will have to register your programs through your instructor. We explain how to do this later in this chapter. You will only have to register the *Merlin* programs once – the first time you open either the *Team Company* or the *Solo Company* programs. You do not need to be connected to the Internet to work with the *Merlin* programs after they have been registered successfully.

Valid Access Code Number

The installation program for *Merlin* requires that you enter the access code number that is found on the flap behind the CD-ROM envelope in the back of this manual. During the installation process, the program will display a screen where you will register and validate the installation of your software. ___If this access number has been used previously, it is invalid. You will NOT be able to use it to install the programs!___ You are limited to installing the *Merlin* programs on **only one** computer for each manual with the CD that you purchase. After you register your access number, it will no longer be valid. **Make sure that you install the programs on the computer you intend to use with the *Merlin* programs before you begin the installation process**. Once you have registered the *Merlin* programs on a particular computer, you will have to purchase another manual with the CD and access code if you wish to use the programs on a different computer.

INSTALLING THE *MERLIN* SOFTWARE

The first time you load the *Merlin – Team* or *Merlin – Solo* program, you must also load certain Windows files that the program needs that may not be in your Windows Systems directory. You will need to run this setup program only once, on each computer you use. After that, just follow the instructions in Chapter 3 for *starting* the *Merlin – Team* or *Merlin – Solo* program. To *load* the *Merlin* Windows files and programs, follow these steps:

1. Load Windows. Open your Windows 95, 98, 2000, ME, or NT program. (Note that this program will not work with Windows 3.1 operating systems.)

2. Close any open applications. Before beginning to load the *Merlin* Windows files, close any applications that are already open or that are opened as part of your Windows startup options. For example, if Microsoft Office automatically loads during your startup of Windows, you will need to close its applications. Closing all applications will prevent conflicts that might arise between files for the *Merlin* program that are being loaded and Windows Systems files currently in use. Do this by closing the applications that are open in the Task Bar displayed across the bottom of your monitor. If your computer automatically loads the MS Office Task Bar (typically found along the side of the monitor or across the top), make sure you close this as well if you experience any difficulties in loading the software.

3. Insert the *Merlin – Team* and *Merlin – Solo* CD into your computer. Click on the Start button and select the **Run** option. Type **d:setup** (*note*: the CD drive for your computer may have a designation other than "d". If your CD drive is *not* "d", substitute the appropriate letter) and click on OK. A message will appear on your monitor to remind you to close all open applications. Select "Cancel" if you have any open applications; otherwise select "Next."

4. Choose Destination Location. Next you will be asked to choose the location where your *Merlin – Team* and *Merlin – Solo* program files will be stored. You will see the dialog box shown in Exhibit 2.1. The default directory and folder is C:\Program Files\Merlin. Unless you need to change this location, select the large button on the left of the dialog box and go to Step 6. If you want to change the folder where you store your program files, go to Step 5.

Exhibit 2.1

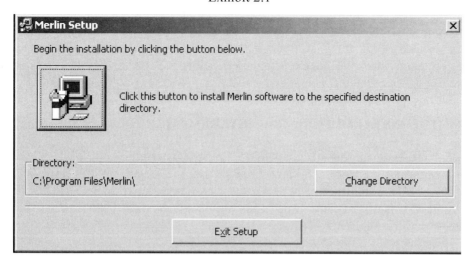

5. Creating a new directory for storing the program files. If you want to create a directory (i.e., folder) with a different name to hold your *Merlin* program files, click on the "Change Directory" button. A screen like Exhibit 2.2 will appear on the monitor. If you do not have a mouse connected to your computer, press the Tab key until you reach this button and then press [ENTER]. Enter the directory name you prefer. You can use any combination of letters and numbers up to a maximum of eight (8) characters. Remember to follow the Windows protocol when creating the location of the new directory. Make sure you have specified the drive where you want to locate the directory, plus the directory's name. For example, if you want to name the directory Merlin2 and have it located in as a program file on Drive C, you would enter **C:\Program Files\Merlin2**.

Exhibit 2.2

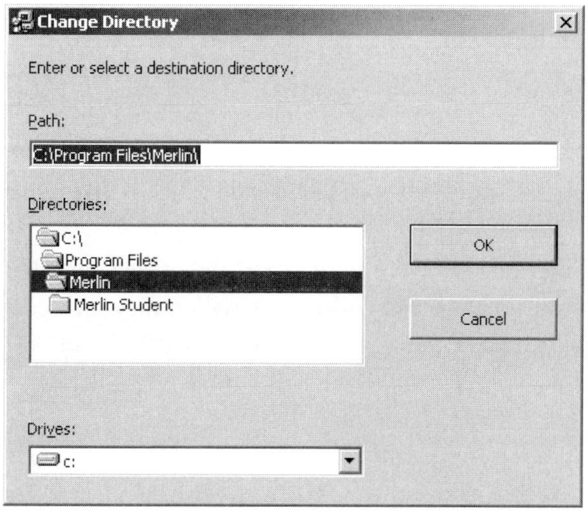

6. Select Program Folder. You will be given the option to change the name of the Program Folder in which the program icons will be stored. Leave this as the default "*Merlin.*"

7. Click on the "Continue" button. The files for *Merlin* will be copied into the folder you selected.

8. <u>Location of the *Merlin* icon</u>. As *Merlin* completes its setup process, it will create icons for the *Merlin Team* and *Merlin Solo* programs. You can access the *Merlin* icon through the "Start" button. To do this, select the "Start" button. A dialogue box will appear on your monitor. Select the icon labeled "Programs." Another dialogue box will appear on your monitor listing the various programs available on that computer. Select the *Merlin* option. Then select the *Solo Company or Team Company* icon to start the desired program.

COMPLETING THE INSTALLATION – REGISTERING MERLIN

As we discussed at the beginning of this chapter, you must register your copy of *Merlin* before you can open and begin working with either the *Solo* or *Team* program. The very first time you start either of the *Merlin* programs (see step 8 above), you will see the dialog box shown in Exhibit 2.3. (Note, you can start the registration process at any time after the software has been loaded by clicking on Start⇨Programs⇨Merlin⇨Register.)

Exhibit 2.3

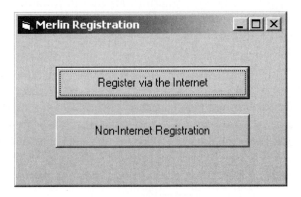

Registering via the Internet

If your computer is connected to the internet and you have Microsoft's Internet Explorer (Version 6.0 or higher) loaded on your computer, select the "Register via the Internet" option. If you do not have access to the internet, click on the bottom option.

If you select "Register via the Internet", you will see a dialog box like that shown in Exhibit 2.4. Fill in the requested information and your access code. You will find your access code behind the CD-ROM envelope in the back of this manual. Finally, click on the "Register" button.

Exhibit 2.4

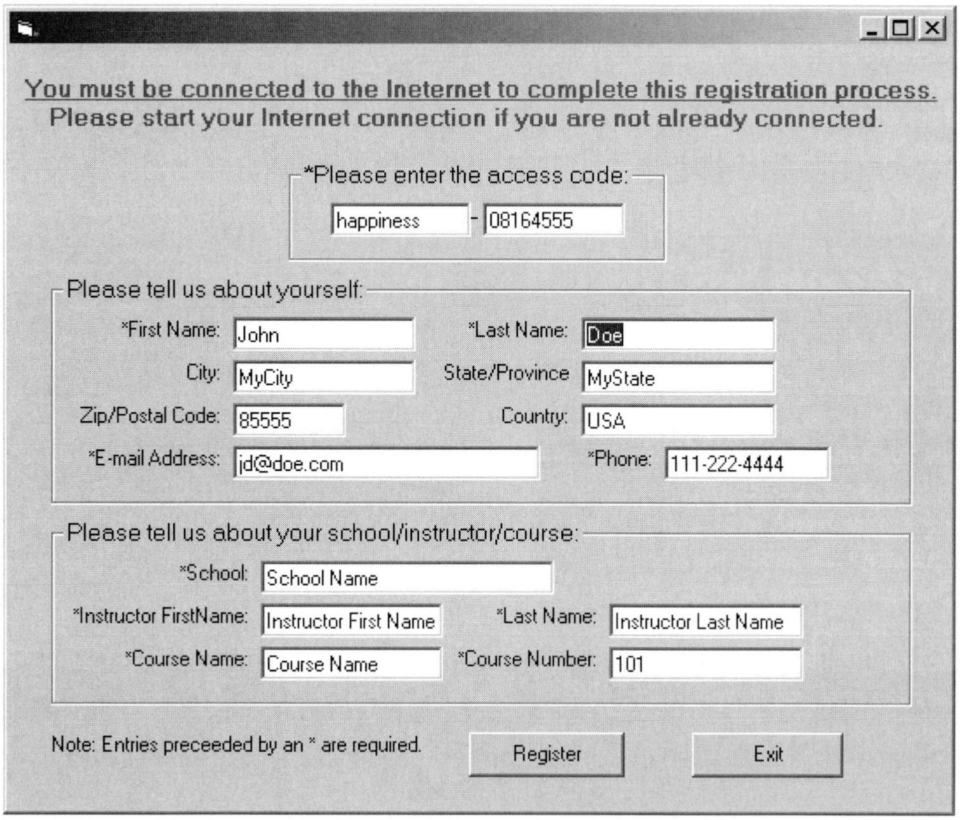

Your access code will be verified and you will see the screen shown in Exhibit 2.5. You are now ready to use the *Merlin* software. You will not have to register the programs again or be connected to the Internet to work with the *Merlin* programs.

Exhibit 2.5

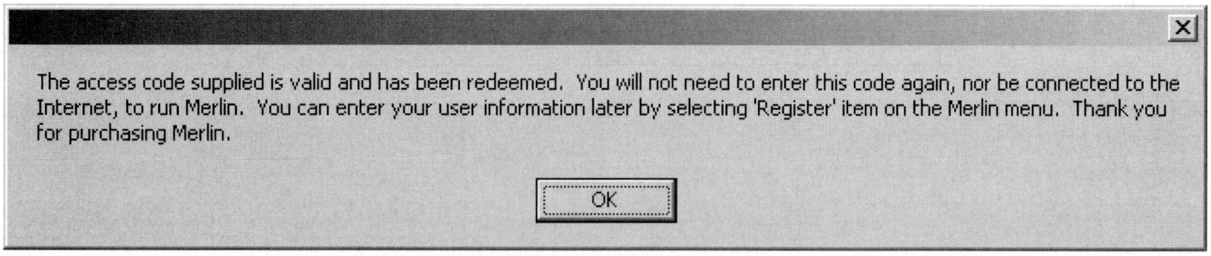

The access code supplied is valid and has been redeemed. You will not need to enter this code again, nor be connected to the Internet, to run Merlin. You can enter your user information later by selecting 'Register' item on the Merlin menu. Thank you for purchasing Merlin.

OK

Note that the access code accompanying your *Merlin* software can be used only one time. If the access code you submit has already been used, you will see a screen like that shown in Exhibit 2.6; you will not be able to get beyond this screen and you will unable to use the *Merlin* software.

If the dialog box tells you that this is not a valid number, or that the number was previously used, you have most likely purchased a used manual. Each access code number is valid for **only one** installation of the software. Return the manual and CD to the bookstore where you purchased it and exchange it for a new manual.

If you get an error message when you click on the "Register" button, see your institution's system administrator to ensure that Microsoft Internet Explorer is installed on your computer and properly configured to access the internet. This is only necessary for **registering** *Merlin*. You do not need to use Internet Explorer or the Internet to **operate** these programs.

Exhibit 2.6

Non-Internet Registration

If your computer is not connected to the internet, you must select the "Non-Internet Registration" button (as shown in Exhibit 2.3). Selecting this option will display a dialog box like that shown in Exhibit 2.7. The *Merlin* software will generate a Registration ID unique for your computer. You must provide your *Merlin* administrator **both** your Registration ID **and** the Access Code that is located behind the CD-ROM envelope in the back of this manual. Your administrator will then provide you with a unique Activation Code for your computer. Enter the Activation Code in the space provided and click on "Activate". (*Note: The Registration ID is case sensitive.*) Your activation information will be verified and you will see the screen shown in Exhibit 2.5. You are now ready to use the *Merlin* software. If you mis-enter the Activation Code in the "Non-Internet Registration" dialog box, you will see the screen shown in Exhibit 2.6.

You can exit the registration procedure without fear at any point short of completion. You can get back to the registration screen by clicking on Start⇨Programs⇨Merlin⇨Register. This will bring you to the screen shown in Exhibit 2.3. When you click on "Non-Internet Registration" the screen shown in Exhibit 2.7 will appear exactly as it did when you left it. Your Registration ID will be exactly the same.

Exhibit 2.7

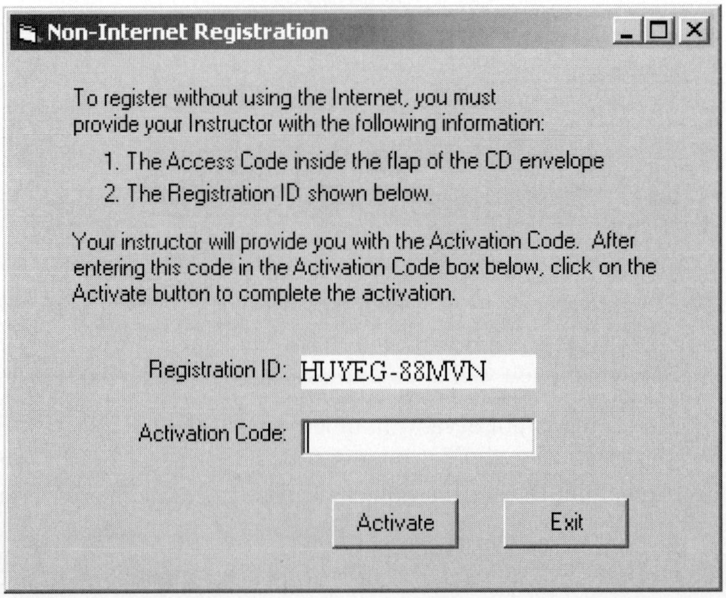

Non-Internet Registration

To register without using the Internet, you must provide your Instructor with the following information:

1. The Access Code inside the flap of the CD envelope
2. The Registration ID shown below.

Your instructor will provide you with the Activation Code. After entering this code in the Activation Code box below, click on the Activate button to complete the activation.

Registration ID: HUYEG-88MVN

Activation Code: [   ]

[Activate]   [Exit]

Note that the access code accompanying your *Merlin* software and the Registration ID can be used only one time. If you give your administrator an access code and ID that has already been used, your administrator will not be able to obtain an Activation Code and you will unable to use the *Merlin* software.

If the dialog box tells you that this is not a valid number, or that the number was previously used, you have most likely purchased a used manual. Each access code number is valid for ***only one*** installation of the software. Return the manual and CD to the bookstore where you purchased it and exchange it for a new manual.

NAVIGATING AROUND *MERLIN*

To work with *Merlin*, you need to be able to move within a screen and among the multiple screens. If you are familiar with working in a Windows environment, the *Merlin* program utilizes standard Windows protocol for keystroke entries. This means the Tab key moves you to the next entry point, the Shift key + Tab key moves you backward to the preceding entry point, and so forth. You can also use a mouse. You can use these two methods in combination with each other, switching back and forth as often as you like. You will use this Windows protocol to move around a screen and make entries. These commands will also allow you to access the Menu bar on your screen. You will use the Menu bar to move among the multiple *Merlin* screens.

In the next chapter we explain in detail how to work with the *Merlin* program. If you are ready to begin working with the program, turn to Chapter 3 now.

CHAPTER 3

WORKING WITH THE *MERLIN* PROGRAM

CHAPTER OVERVIEW

This chapter will introduce you to the *Merlin* program. It will explain how to:
- Work with the *Merlin* program, either with or without a mouse.
- Make entries on the four decisions screens.
- Move from one screen to another screen using (a) the [PgDn] and [PgUp] keys, (b) the Menu bar displayed across the top of every screen, or (c) the *Merlin* "hot" keys.
- Use the Menu bar to perform various operations.

After reading this chapter, you should be familiar with the mechanics of working with the *Merlin* software. In the next chapter, we discuss the decisions you will make to manage your *Merlin* company.

Whether you will be using the team or the solo version of *Merlin* we recommend that you use *Merlin Solo* as a tool to learn the fundamentals of working with the *Merlin* program. Use *Merlin Solo* to try out each step as you read about it. Do not worry about what decisions you enter. Any of the decisions you enter now can be changed later. If you cannot get access to a computer as you read this chapter, you will still be able to understand the information presented here. Read the text and look at the sample screens in the text to see what you will see on the computer monitor. Then try everything out on a computer as soon as possible.

MERLIN TEAM AND *MERLIN SOLO* DIFFERENCES

As explained in Chapter 1, *Merlin Team* and *Merlin Solo* are two versions of the same program. The decisions you enter and the reports created by the programs are identical. In the *Merlin Team* program, your competition will be companies managed by other simulation participants. In the *Merlin Solo* program, your competition will be eleven companies managed by the computer. While the decisions and the reports associated with the two programs are the same, there are two differences that we will highlight in this chapter.

Processing Decisions

The *Merlin Team* and *Merlin Solo* programs differ in how the decisions you enter are processed. If you need to refresh your memory on this issue, reread the section in Chapter 1 on how the two programs work. When you get to the section in this chapter that deals with processing, we will discuss the differences between *Merlin Team* and *Merlin Solo* in detail.

Storing Your Company Data File – Floppy versus Hard Drive

Both *Merlin Team* and *Merlin Solo* require that you create and save a company data file for storing your decisions. For both the *Team* and *Solo* versions of *Merlin* you can choose to run the simulation with either a floppy disk or your computer's hard disk. Which to use depends on the format desired by your simulation administrator and on how often you will be submitting your *Merlin* work. Most administrators will ask you to submit decisions for the team version of *Merlin* on a disk. If you will be submitting your work frequently or are uncomfortable with your ability to copy files from the hard disk to a floppy disk, we recommend that you use a floppy disk for storing your company data file. Otherwise use the hard disk, as it provides faster processing of a quarter's decisions. **It is imperative that you remember where you store (i.e., save) your company data file. If you exit the program and forget where the file is located, you will be unable to access the information you need to process future decisions. (If you are playing *Merlin Solo,* you will have to start from the beginning the next time you work with the program!)**

Starting the Programs

Remember that you will not be able to use either *Merlin Team* or *Merlin Solo* unless you have first *installed* and *registered* the software. See Chapter 2 for the installation and registration instructions. Remember also that you are limited to installing the *Merlin* programs **only one time** on **only one computer** for each CD that you purchase. Once the access number on the CD has been used, it is no longer valid and you will not be able to register or operate the *Merlin* programs.)

Because there are separate programs for *Merlin Team* and *Merlin Solo*, the procedure for starting each program is different. With the exceptions of how to start the programs and how to process your decision entries, *Merlin Team* and *Merlin Solo* are identical in their operation.

Remember, you need to have previously loaded the *Merlin* Windows files on *the machine on which you are working* before you are able to use the *Merlin* programs. If you have not done this, you will get an error message similar to that shown in Exhibit 3.1. Go to Chapter 2 and follow the directions for loading the *Merlin* programs onto this computer.

Exhibit 3.1

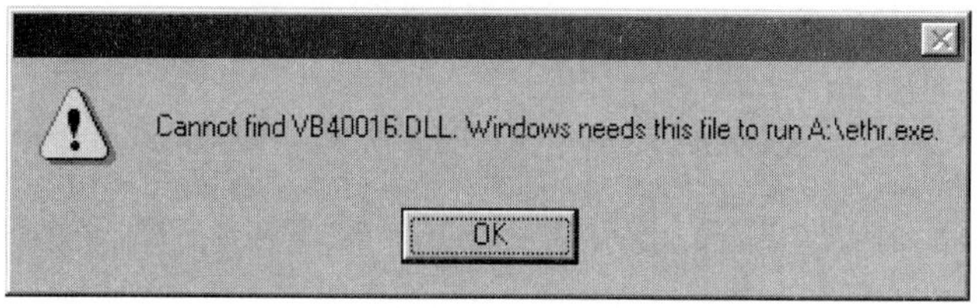

STARTING THE *MERLIN SOLO* PROGRAM

1. To start the *Merlin* program, select the "Start" button. A dialogue box will appear on your monitor. Select the "Programs" option. Another dialogue box will appear on your monitor listing the various programs available on that computer. Select the *Merlin* option. Then select the *Solo* company icon to start the program. (*Remember that the very first time you start either* Merlin Team *or* Merlin Solo, *you must go through the registration process. See Chapter 2 for registration instructions.* Keep in mind that you cannot register or operate the *Merlin* programs on your computer if the software has been registered on another computer.)

2. Wait while the computer loads *Merlin Solo*. Assuming you have registered the *Merlin* software, you will see the opening title screen for *Merlin Solo*. Press any key to begin working with the program.

3. The screen shown in Exhibit 3.2 will appear. Select the "Create New Industry" button and click on OK.

Exhibit 3.2

4. You will now see a dialog box that will prompt you for your company name and password. The dialog box is shown in Exhibit 3.3.

Exhibit 3.3

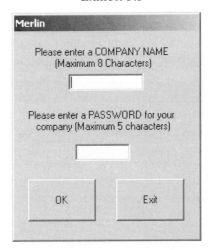

Enter a company name and password and select the OK button. Exhibit 3.4 describes issues you should consider when choosing your company name and password.

Exhibit 3.4

Entering a Company Name. Think of a name that you would like to call your company. This name can be any combination of letters or numbers up to a maximum of eight (8) characters. In this example, we will use the company name "demo". There is no relationship between your company name and the success or failure of your company, so select any name that you desire. Type in this name and press the Tab key. This action will move the cursor to the cell for entering a password for your *Merlin* disk.

Entering a Password. Think of a password for your company that you can remember easily. Your password can have a maximum of five (5) characters. It is advisable not to select a password others are likely to guess such as a nickname or the name of a family member. Type in your password. Then press the Tab key until the OK button is highlighted and press [ENTER] or click on the OK button if you are using a mouse.

Once you have done this, you will have to enter this password whenever you start the *Merlin Solo* program. If the correct password is not entered, the program will not proceed. If you forget your password, you will have to take your company disk to your administrator to have it read. If you desire, you can change your company's password and your company name later in the simulation exercise. We explain how to make these changes later in this chapter under "Menu Bar Operations."

Make sure you protect your password and your *Merlin* company data file. If other players find your company data file in a computer and know your password, you give them access to all your company's records. You would no more want to do this than to give them printouts of your company reports. You do not want them to benefit from your hard work.

5. Next, you must select the location for your company's data file. This location will determine where (a) the data file will be stored (i.e., saved) after you create it and (b) where you will find an existing company data file that you created earlier. We discuss how to create an existing company data file next. Later in this chapter (in the section entitled **Locating an Existing Company Data File**) we explain how to retrieve an existing company data file that contains results from decisions you made during an earlier working session. The default location for saving your *Merlin Solo* file is the directory in which you stored the program files (usually Program Files\Merlin) when you installed *Merlin*. (See Chapter 2.) Exhibit 3.5 shows how this screen looks.

Exhibit 3.5

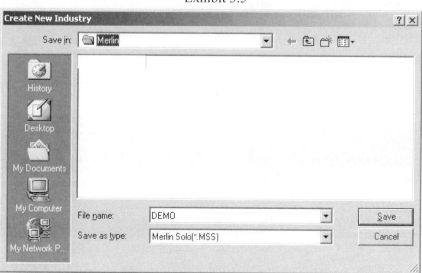

If you wish to run *Merlin Solo* from your hard drive, you may accept this default location. However, if you would rather run *Merlin Solo* from a floppy disk, you must change this default designation to the floppy drive. (There is a discussion of the advantages and disadvantages of using the hard drive versus the floppy on earlier in this chapter, **Storing Your Company Data File – Floppy versus Hard Drive**). If you wish to save your company data file on a floppy disk, you must first insert a blank, formatted disk in your floppy drive (Drive A or B). Make sure that you put your name on the disk. You can now switch the destination of your *Merlin Solo* company data file to your floppy drive (Drive A or B) by selecting the ▼, then choosing A (or B). *Note: If you designate the floppy drive without having a formatted disk in the drive, a box will appear stating that your floppy drive is not accessible, the device is not ready.*

6. Select "Save" and your company data files will be stored at your chosen location and you will see a screen like that shown in Exhibit 3.6. (Note: The *Merlin Solo* program names your company data file by adding a ".MSS" extension to the name you chose when you saved the file. In this example, the company data file is DEMO.MSS. When you work with a *Merlin Team* program it will add a "MTS" extension to your company data file name.) If you have chosen to save your *Merlin Solo* company data file on a floppy, this saving operation will take from 20 to 30 seconds, depending on the speed of your computer. This is because the program has to create a large file on your company disk. This long delay occurs only when you *create* a new game. Once this file has been created, it will take only a few seconds to load your company data file when you next start the program. Once the program has loaded the company data file, you will be able to enter decisions and view your company's results.

Exhibit 3.6

Decisions - Product 1		Territory 1	Territory 2	Territory 3
Price	($)	19.00	19.00	19.00
Newspaper Ads	(#)	15	15	15
Consumer Magazine Ads	(#)	10	10	10
Trade magazine Ads	(#)	12	12	12
Ad Message		Service ▼	Service ▼	Service ▼
Sales Reps:				
Hire	(#)	0	0	0
Fire	(#)	0	0	0
Commission	(%)	3	3	3
Product Quality	($/Unit)	0.00	(For all territories)	
Web Spending	($)	8000	(For all territories and both products)	
Sales Forecast	(#)	31800	14600	39600
Product Ordered	(#)	55000	25000	65000
Product Features Development	($)	0		
Process Improvement	($)	0		
ST Loan Request	($)	700000		

SOLO Industry - Merlin SOLO - Q 1 FORECAST - DEMO Company 1

File   Quarter   Decisions   Reports   Info   Print   Windows

STARTING THE *MERLIN TEAM* PROGRAM

Remember, you need to have previously loaded the *Merlin* Windows files on *the machine on which you are working* before you are able to use the *Merlin* programs. If you have not done this, you will get an error message similar to that shown in Exhibit 3.1. Go to Chapter 2 and follow the directions for loading the *Merlin* programs onto this computer.

Running the *Merlin Team* with Your Company Data File on a Floppy Disk

If you are participating in the team version of *Merlin*, your simulation administrator will provide you with the data file (usually on a floppy disk) that you need for starting the simulation. If your company data file is on a floppy disk, insert your disk in Drive A (or Drive B, if that is your floppy drive). It is easiest if you insert your disk into the floppy drive *before* you start the *Merlin* program.

Next, start the *Merlin* program by selecting the "Start" button. A dialogue box will appear on your monitor. Select the "Programs" option. Another dialogue box will appear on your monitor listing the various programs available on that computer. Select the *Merlin* option. Then select the *Merlin Team* company icon to start the program. (*Remember that the very first time you start either* Merlin Team *or* Merlin Solo, *you must go through the registration process. See Chapter 2 for registration instructions.* Keep in mind that you cannot register or operate the *Merlin* programs on your computer if the software has been registered on another computer.)

Wait while the computer loads *Merlin Team*. You will see the opening title screen for *Merlin Team*. Press any key to begin working with the program. If your company disk was in your floppy drive when you started *Merlin*, you will see a dialog box like that shown in Exhibit 3.7. Click OK and the *Merlin* program will start.

Exhibit 3.7

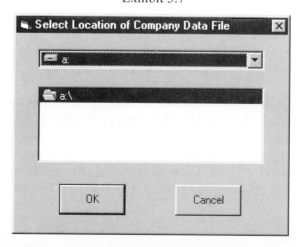

NOTE: If your company disk was not in the floppy drive when you started the program, the dialog box shown in Figure 3.8 will appear. To run *Merlin* from the floppy drive, you must insert your company disk in the floppy drive (Drive A or B) and then select the floppy drive by clicking on the ▼ , then choosing A (or B). When you see the dialog box shown in Exhibit 3.7, click OK and the *Merlin* program will start.

Exhibit 3.8

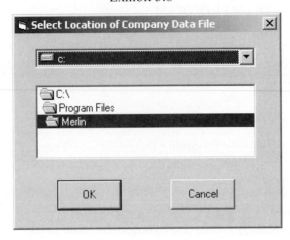

The first time you start the *Merlin* program, a screen will appear asking you to provide a company name and password. See Exhibit 3.3 above for the dialog box and Exhibit 3.4 for advice on choosing a company name and password. Once you have entered your company name and password you will see a screen like that shown in Exhibit 3.6.

Running *Merlin Team* with Your Company Data File on the Hard Disk

If you wish to run *Merlin* from the hard drive of your computer, you must copy your company data file into a folder on the hard drive. This copying operation is most easily accomplished using Windows Explorer. If you are unfamiliar with the procedure for copying files, we recommend that you operate *Merlin Team* using the floppy disk option described above.

Once you have your company data file in a folder on the hard drive, start the *Merlin* program by selecting the "Start" button. A dialogue box will appear on your monitor. Select the "Programs" option. Another dialogue box will appear on your monitor listing the various programs available on that computer. Select the *Merlin* option. Then select the *Merlin Team* company icon to start the program. Wait while the computer loads *Merlin Team*. You will see the opening title screen for *Merlin Team*. Press any key to begin working with the program.

It is easiest if there is *no* disk in the floppy drive when you start the *Merlin* program. If the floppy drive is empty, the program will automatically look for your company data file in the same folder (i.e., directory) in which you stored your *Merlin* program during the setup process. If you decide to store your company data file in a different location on the hard drive, you must select that folder by clicking on the ▼ and then choosing the proper location. Exhibit 3.9 shows how the dialog box would look if you had stored your company data file in a folder named "Example".

Exhibit 3.9

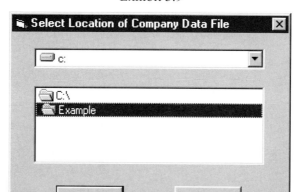

Note: If you start *Merlin Team* with a disk in the floppy drive, you will see a dialog box like that shown in Exhibit 3.7. You will have to switch to the location of your company data file by clicking on the ▼, and selecting the appropriate folder.

Once you have designated the folder containing you company data file, click OK. The first time you start the *Merlin Team* program, a screen will appear asking you to provide a company name and password. See Exhibit 3.3 above for the dialog box and Exhibit 3.4 for advice on choosing a company name and password. Once you have entered your company name and password you will see a screen like that shown in Exhibit 3.6.

LOCATING AN EXISTING COMPANY DATA FILE

Since the procedure for locating an existing company data file is a bit different for *Merlin Solo* than for *Merlin Team*, we'll discuss each separately.

Opening an <u>Existing</u> *Merlin <u>Solo</u>* Company Data File

Once the program for *Merlin* has loaded and you have moved past the opening title screen, the screen shown in Exhibit 3.2 will appear. Select "Open Existing Industry" and click OK. The program will automatically look for the company data file in the same folder (i.e., directory) in which you stored your *Merlin* program during the setup process – usually Program Files\Merlin. If you stored your data file in this folder, your company data file name will appear in the dialog box. Select the data file and click on the "Open" button.

If your company data file is stored in a different location, you will have to switch to that location by clicking on the ▼, and selecting the appropriate folder. For example, if your company data file is named "Demo" and is stored on a floppy disk, you would click on the ▼, select the A (or B) drive, highlight "DEMO" and click open. You would then see a screen like that shown in Exhibit 3.10.

Exhibit 3.10

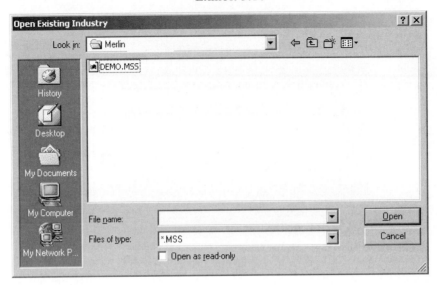

When you have completed this task, you will be prompted for your password. (See Exhibit 3.11.) Note that you are not asked for your company name as was the case when you entered the program the first time. When you enter you enter your password and click OK, you will see a screen similar to that shown in Exhibit 3.6.

Exhibit 3.11

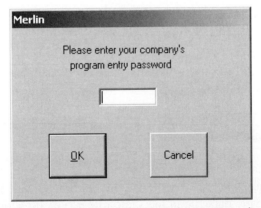

If you are at an incorrect location using *Merlin Solo* (and the program is unable to find the data file, for example DEMO.MSS) you will *not* be able to retrieve your existing company file. If you want to play *Merlin Solo*, **you will have to begin the game from the beginning!** You need to know the location of your most current company data file, if you intend to use it again. **Do not forget where you save your most current company data file.**

Opening an <u>Existing</u> *Merlin <u>Team</u>* Company Data File

Once the program for *Merlin* has loaded and you have moved past the opening title screen, you must specify the location of your company data file. If you have a disk in your floppy drive when you load the program *Merlin Team* will assume that you are operating the simulation from a floppy disk and you will see a screen like that shown in Exhibit 3.12.

Exhibit 3.12

If company data file is on the floppy, simply click on OK and you will be prompted for your company password. (See Exhibit 3.11.) If your company data file is stored in another location, click on the ▼, and select the appropriate folder.

If there is no disk in the floppy drive when you start *Merlin Team*, the program will default to the hard disk folder where the program is stored – usually Program Files\Merlin. If this is where you stored the data file, select OK. If you saved the file elsewhere on your hard drive, you must first change to that location and then select OK.

If you are working with *Merlin Team* and you select a location that does not contain your *Merlin* company's data file (MP.MTS), you will see the following message, "Can't find Company Data File(MP.MTS) – Unable to continue." You need to know the location of your most current company data file, if you intend to use it again. **Do not forget where you save your most current company data file.**

USING THE *MERLIN* PROGRAM

Once you have loaded and registered *Merlin Solo* or *Merlin Team* you will see the opening title screen. Press any key and the screen asking for your password will come up. Once you have entered your password you will see a screen that looks like Exhibit 3.6, shown above.

This is the first of four screens that your team will use to enter its decisions for Quarter 1 and subsequent quarters as you move through the simulation exercise. What follows is a preview of *Merlin* that describes how to enter decisions, move around a decision screen, and move from one screen to another screen.

Merlin has two screens you will use to enter your decisions for the marketing mix of your two products. You will also use these screens to enter decisions regarding product development, to order products from a sub-contractor, and to finance your decisions. See Exhibits 3.6 and 3.13 for examples of these screens. You will notice that Exhibit 3.6 and 3.13 are very similar. Exhibit 3.6 is the screen for Product 1 while Exhibit 3.13 is the screen for Product 2. The screen for Product 1 (Exhibit 3.6) has two entries not contained on the screen for Product 2 – a Short Term Loan Request and a slot for Web Spending.

Exhibit 3.13

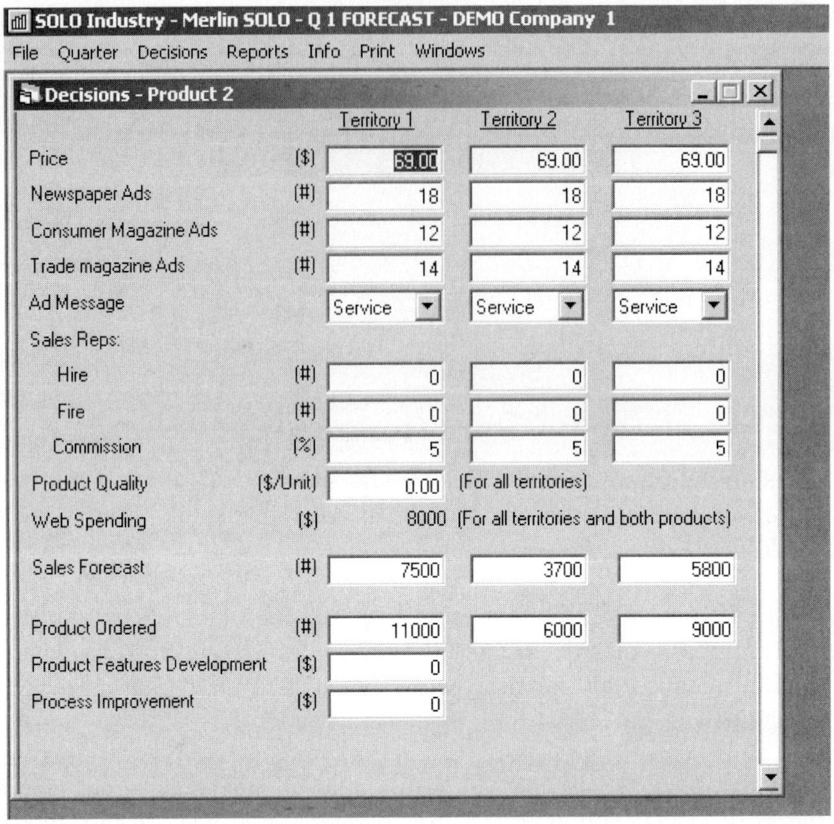

There are two additional screens (one for Product 1 and one for Product 2) that you will use to enter marketing research decisions to gather information about your competitors and the industry-wide demand for the two products. Exhibit 3.16 shows an example of what these two screens look like.

In addition to these four decision screens, there are a number of screens that display reports showing the results of the decisions you made. The decision screens will have a flashing cursor to guide you in entering your decisions. You cannot make entries on any of the report screens. Consequently, there is no need to move the cursor around those screens.

Entering a Decision

The *Merlin* program will only allow you to make certain entries in specific locations. This is to prevent you from making entry mistakes. If you attempt an invalid entry (e.g., a number that exceeds the decision limits or entering a letter where a number is required), the *Merlin* program will indicate this by displaying an error message on the screen. You can access information on the costs for various decisions through the Info heading on the Menu bar, or by using certain *Merlin* "hot" keys. We will explain just how to view this information later in this chapter. You can find the acceptable limits for *Merlin* decisions in Appendix F of this manual.

Saving Your Decisions

The *Merlin* program saves any entries you make whenever you select the Save & Exit option. *If you either shut off the computer or remove the disk before saving and exiting the program, any changes that you made during your session with Merlin will be lost!* Therefore, it is very important that you select Save & Exit when you are finished with your session. As will be explained later, you can always change any entries you have made and saved onto your disk up to the time the quarter's decisions are processed. Once your decisions for a quarter have been processed, you can no longer change them.

Correcting an Error

If you make a mistake or want to change something you have typed, simply move to the number you want to change using either the Tab key or the mouse. Type in your new decision and press the Tab key. This will replace the old number with your new number.

MOVING THE CURSOR AROUND THE DECISION SCREENS

You can move the cursor around the two decision screens by either of two methods. One method is to use the Tab key. The second method is to use the mouse. You can use each of these methods in combination with the other method. This means you can make one move using the mouse and the next move using the Tab key. You can switch back and forth between these two methods of moving around a decision screen as often as you like. Each of the two methods is described briefly in the following two sections.

Using the Tab Key

When the decision screen first appears, a flashing cursor will appear next to the first decision you must make — the price of Product l. Use the Tab key to move from decision to decision on the screen. Pressing the Tab key alone will move you "forward" to the next decision entry cell. Pressing and holding the Shift key and then pressing the Tab key will move you "backward" to the preceding decision entry cell. When you reach the last decision on the screen, pressing the Tab key will take you back to the first decision on the screen. You can enter the individual decisions in any order you choose. What matters is the last set of numbers showing on the screen after you have finished entering your decisions.

If you do not want to change the number shown on the screen, press the Tab key to move to the next decision you must make. This will automatically enter the number displayed on the screen. If you wish to make a change, simply type in your new number (or letter) and press the Tab key. This will enter your new number (or letter) and move you to the next decision. Notice that when you tab to a new cell, the whole cell is highlighted. If you press the Backspace key, the whole number is erased. You must then enter a new number and press the Tab key, or the *Merlin* program will automatically enter a zero for that decision.

If you press an Arrow key while the number is highlighted, the highlighting will disappear, but the number will remain. You can then use the Arrow key to move to a digit within the number and make a change to the existing number without having to change the whole number. For example, you could change a sales forecast number from 16,100 to 16,150. To *insert* a digit into an existing number, use the Arrow key to move to the insertion point, type in the new digit, use the Delete or the Backspace key to remove any unwanted digit(s), and press the Tab key. To *type over* a particular digit, use the Arrow key to move to the digit you want to replace, press the Insert key, then type in the new digit and tab to the next decision cell. Notice how the shape of the flashing cursor changes after you press the Insert key. Once you have pressed the Insert key, you will be able to type over existing numbers until you press the Insert key again and the flashing cursor returns to its original shape.

Using the Mouse

Use the mouse to move around a decisions screen the same as you would when working in any Windows environment. Simply move the mouse indicator to the decision number you want to change and click the left mouse button. The number you selected will become highlighted. Type in the number you desire and either press the Tab key or click on a new number. Repeat this process until you have made all the changes you desire to the decisions showing on the screen.

Clicking twice on a number will allow you to edit the existing number on the screen. The first click highlights the number. The second click positions the cursor in the number so that you can type in a digit and delete unwanted digits using the Backspace or Delete keys. As with working without a mouse, pressing the Insert key allows you to type over existing numbers.

You will need to enter information on four screens — the two decisions screens plus the two marketing research screens. If you are at the computer, try entering some information on the Marketing and Market Research Decisions screen now. None of the numbers you enter at this time will become permanent. Even during the simulation exercise, no decision is permanent until you process the quarter's decisions. This means the only numbers that matter are the *last* ones entered before your quarter's decisions are processed. So feel free to experiment now. Chapter 6 explains each of the decisions you will enter on the four decision screens.

MOVING FROM SCREEN TO SCREEN

Merlin has a number of screens that you can view and/or print out when working on the exercise. These are: (a) the decision screens, on which you enter your decisions, (b) the reports screens, where you can see the results of decisions you have made, and (c) the information screens, which provide you with information on various parts of *Merlin*, such as the costs of your operations.

There are three methods that you can use for moving from screen to screen. One method is to use the Menu bar displayed across the top of the *Merlin* screens. The second method is to use a combination of the [PgUp] and [PgDn] keys. The third method is to use the *Merlin* "hot" keys to move directly to a decision, report, or information screen. We will now discuss each of the three methods, in turn.

Using the Menu Bar

You can access each of the reports/screens listed above through the Menu bar. The Menu bar is always shown across the top of your screen, regardless of what particular screen you are viewing. There are seven headings listed on the Menu bar. They are File, Quarter, Decisions, Reports, Info, Print and Windows. Under each of these headings are a number of options that you can use. For example, as shown in Exhibit 3.14, if you are working with *Merlin Solo*, under the File heading you have the option to (a) Open Existing Industry, (b) Create New Industry, (c) Process Industry (d) Create Company Spreadsheet, (e) Create Performance Spreadsheet (f) Select Quarter, (g) Change Password, (h) Change Company Name, and (i) Save & Exit. We will discuss each of these options, in detail, later.

Exhibit 3.14

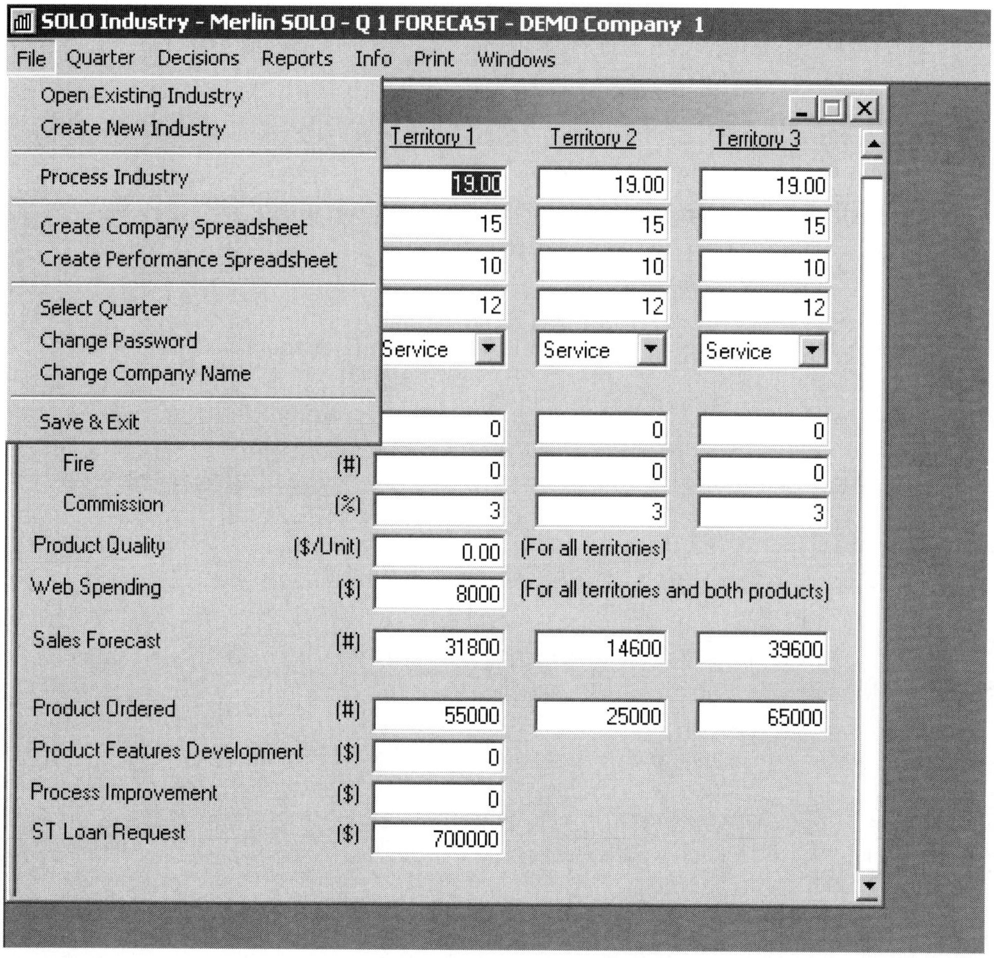

There are two methods you can use to access each of the headings on the Menu bar and the options associated with each heading. One method is to use a mouse; the other is to use a combination of the [ALT] and Arrow keys. As with the decision screens, you can use each of these methods in combination with the other method. We describe both methods for accessing the Menu bar next.

Using the Mouse. To access a heading on the Menu bar using the mouse, simply click on the heading with which you want to work. The options available for that heading are automatically displayed. To select an option, just click on it with the mouse.

Using the [ALT] and Arrow Keys. To access the Menu bar, press the [ALT] key. Notice that the heading labeled as "File" becomes highlighted. Notice also that the first letter in each of the other headings is underlined. Press the → and ← arrow keys to move to the other headings on the Menu bar. You can also move directly to a heading by pressing the letter that is underlined for each option.

To access the options under each heading, press the ↓ (i.e., down) arrow key. A list of options available under that heading will appear on your screen. To select one of these options, press the down arrow key until your desired option is highlighted and press [ENTER]. Alternatively, each one of the options will have a letter that is underlined. Pressing that letter on your keyboard will also select that option. Each of the options available through the Menu bar headings will be discussed later in this chapter. For now, concentrate on the mechanics of moving from screen to screen using the Menu bar.

Notice that once the options for a particular heading have been displayed, pressing an Arrow key to move to the next heading will automatically display the options for that heading. The options for the headings will continue to remain displayed until you press either the [ALT] key again or the ESC key.

Using the [PgUp] and [PgDn] Keys

To move from screen to screen using the [PgUp] and [PgDn] keys, press:
- [PgUp]   to move back to the previous screen.
- [PgDn]   to move to the next screen.

Press [PgDn] to see the next screen. You should now see the second decision screen, the Product 2 Decisions screen (Exhibit 3.15).

Exhibit 3.15

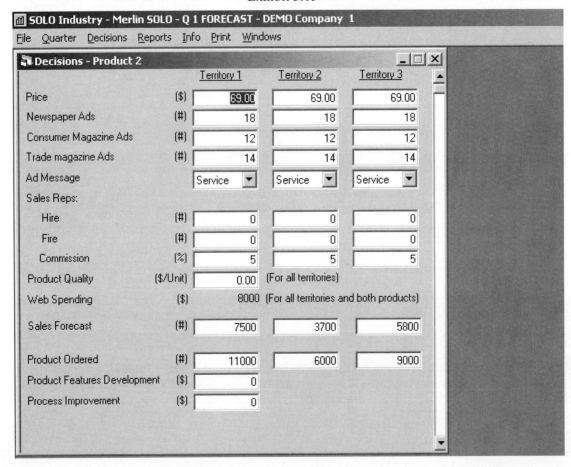

Press [PgDn] again. This time you will see the marketing research decision screen for Product 1 (see Exhibit 3.16). Entering decisions on this screen, and on the marketing research decision screen for Product 2, will be explained in detail in Chapter 6.

Exhibit 3.16

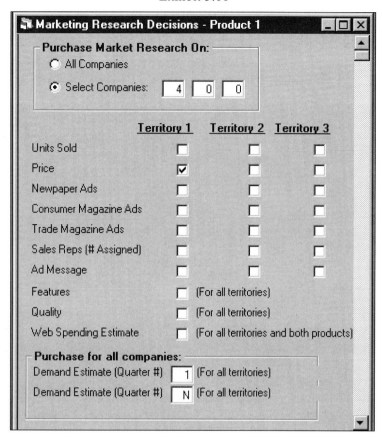

The Report Screens. Press [PgDn] again. This time you will see the first of the reports screens, the Product Cost Report (see Exhibit 3.17). We will explain this and the other reports screens in Chapter 7. Continue pressing [PgDn] to see the rest of the reports. The reports appear in the following sequence:

- Product Cost Report
- Inventory Report
- Product 1 Report
- Product 2 Report
- Sales & Admin Summary Report
- Income Statement
- Balance Sheet
- Cash Flow Statement
- Market Research P1
- Market Research P2
- Quarter Performance Report (Actual results only. Not shown for Forecast reports.)
- Game-to-Date Performance Report (Actual results only. Not shown for Forecast reports.)
- Cost Parameters Report
- Bulletin

Exhibit 3.17

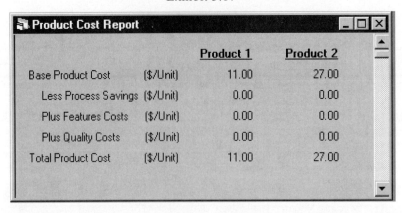

If you are working on the computer, try pressing [PgDn] and [PgUp] a number of times until you are familiar with their operation.

Using *Merlin* "Hot" Keys

In addition to using a combination of the [PgUp] and [PgDn] keys or the Menu bar, the *Merlin* program also has a number of "hot" keys that let you to move from one screen directly to another screen, regardless of where you are in the program. For example, pressing the F1 key moves you directly to the Product 1 Decision screen. You can also use "hot" keys to move directly to any of the reports. To do this, press and hold the [CTRL] key, then press the letter or function key listed under the Reports Menu option. For example, if you press and hold the [CTRL] key and press C, the Cash Flow Statement will appear on the monitor.

Appendix G provides a listing of these special "hot" keys for *Merlin*. These "hot" keys are also listed with their associated reports or screens when you access the options under the heading on the Menu bar. The Menu bar appears at the top of all screens when you use the *Merlin* program.

This means you are not limited to using the [PgUp] and [PgDn] keys or the Menu bar to move from one screen to another screen. However, if you have pressed the [ALT] key and highlighted the Menu bar, the "hot" keys are disabled. They will not work while you are using the Menu bar options. Pressing [ESC] will take you out of the Menu bar and enable the "hot" keys for your use. Learning to use the *Merlin* "hot" keys allows you to move quickly around the program and can shorten the time necessary to make a decision.

You now should know how to move around the decisions screens and to move from one screen to another. Next we will describe what each of the options under the Menu bar headings can do.

MENU BAR OPERATIONS

As mentioned earlier, the Menu bar contains seven headings: File, Quarter, Decisions, Reports, Info, Print and Windows. Using the Menu bar will allow you to work with your *Merlin* files. You will be able to enter decisions for managing your company, view reports on your company's operation, access information regarding *Merlin*, and print out any, or all, of the screens you can view. Each of these is discussed below.

The File Menu

The operations that you can perform using the File menu depend upon whether you are working with the Team version or the Solo version of *Merlin*. As shown in Exhibit 3.14, *Merlin Solo* has nine different options. These are: (a) Open Existing Industry, (b) Create New Industry, (c) Process Industry (d) Create Company Spreadsheet, (e) Create Performance Spreadsheet (f) Select Quarter, (g) Change Password, (h) Change Company Name, and (i) Save & Exit. *Merlin Team* has only six options. *Merlin Team* does not permit you to Open Existing Industry nor to Create New Industry, so these two options do not appear as menu choices. (See Exhibit 3.18 for the differences in the pull down menus for *Merlin Solo* and *Merlin Team*.) In addition, if you are using *Merlin Team*, you cannot process the results for a quarter; the simulation administrator processes each quarter's decisions. Each of these options will be discussed in order.

Exhibit 3.18

File options using:

Merlin Solo

| File | Quarter | Decisions | Reports | Ir |

Open Existing Industry
Create New Industry

Process Industry

Create Company Spreadsheet
Create Performance Spreadsheet

Select Quarter
Change Password
Change Company Name

Save & Exit

Merlin Team

| File | Quarter | Decisions | Reports | Ir |

Create Company Spreadsheet
Create Performance Spreadsheet

Select Quarter
Change Password
Change Company Name

Save & Exit

Open Existing Industry (Available only for *Merlin Solo*). The usual way to open an existing game is to choose "Open Existing Industry" when you first enter *Merlin Solo* (see Exhibit 3.2). The "Open Existing Industry" option on the pull-down menu under the File heading is simply an alternative means of starting an existing game. When you choose this option, you will see a dialog box prompting you for the location of your company data file. Follow the instructions for "Locating an existing company data file" earlier in this chapter.

Create New Industry (Available only for *Merlin Solo*). The usual way to create a new game is to choose "Create New Industry" when you first enter *Merlin Solo* (see Exhibit 3.2). However, you can also start a new game from the pull-down menu under the File heading. If you are playing the *Solo* simulation and decide that you do not want to continue the game you are in, you can choose Create New Industry from the pull-down menu to begin a new game at Quarter 1. Whenever you start a new game, *Merlin Solo* creates new industry-wide demand schedules for your two products. It also resets the relative importance of the marketing variables for determining the market share captured as a result of your marketing efforts. Lastly, it selects a new set of weights for the performance criteria reported in the two performance reports. Chapter 7 will discuss these factors in detail. For now, it is only important for you to recognize that each time you start a new game things will be different from the game you were playing. For example, the demand for your products may differ and the influence of newspaper advertising in determining sales may increase or decrease.

When you select the Create New Industry option, a dialog will appear on your screen prompting you for a new company name and password.

Process Industry (Available only for *Merlin Solo*). After making your forecasts and finalizing your decisions for a quarter, you can process your decisions by selecting the Process Industry option. You should choose this option only *after* you are satisfied with your decisions and want to see the results these decisions will achieve. When you select Process Industry, a dialog box will appear (see Exhibit 3.19) asking you to confirm that you wish to process your decisions and proceed to the next quarter (e.g., move from Quarter 1 to Quarter 2). Click on "Yes" when the dialogue box appears on your monitor. Once you say "Yes," the program will process Quarter 1's decisions and move forward to Quarter 2.

Exhibit 3.19

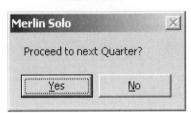

To view or print your Actual Results and Standings for Quarter 1, choose the Select Quarter option under the File heading, as will be discussed shortly. Enter a "1" in the dialogue box that appears on your monitor. When you finish reviewing your results and are ready to proceed to Quarter 2 to enter decisions, choose the Select Quarter option and enter a "2." Repeat this process for each subsequent quarter of play. You can also change to a different quarter by using the Quarter Menu, which we will discuss later.

Create Company Spreadsheet. Selecting this option automatically creates an Excel spreadsheet of your decisions. *NOTE: You will be unable to create a company spreadsheet until after at least one quarter has been processed.* If you select this option before at least one quarter has been processed, a men box will pop up stating, "You cannot use this function until after Quarter 1 is processed."

When you choose this option you will see the following dialog box (see Exhibit 3.20). As the dialog box shows, the spreadsheet is saved in a file named CompData in the Program Files\Merlin folder. To open the file, start up Excel (Start⇨Programs⇨Microsoft Excel). Then, since the spreadsheet is saved as a "csv" file, you must click on the ▼ for Files of Type: and select All Files (*.*). When you do this, the CompData file will appear in the dialog box. Click "Open" and the CompData spreadsheet will open.

The CompData spreadsheet contains data for much of your own internal company operations – the prices you set for each of your products in each territory, the number of ads you ran, the number of units you sold, your ending inventory, etc. Appendix H provides a listing of the contents of the CompData file. You may find the CompData very helpful in tracking your decisions as well as some of your outcomes (process savings, number of features achieved, quality expenditures, unit sales, and inventory levels) over the course of the simulation. You may wish to examine the contents of the file, or better yet, to plot the variables to monitor your performance.

Exhibt 3.20

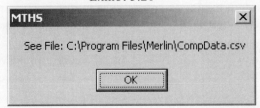

Create Performance Spreadsheet. Selecting this option produces an Excel spreadsheet for many of the components of your Quarter Performance and Game to Date Performance Reports. That is, the spreadsheet contains information on the sales, income, and return on sales for all competitors in your industry. As with the Company Data spreadsheet, you will be unable to create a company spreadsheet until after at least one quarter has been processed. If you select this option before at least one quarter has been processed, a men box will pop up stating, "You cannot use this function until after Quarter 1 is processed."

When you choose this option, the dialog box shown in Exhibit 3.21 will appear. As the dialog box shows, the spreadsheet is saved in a file named PerfData in the Program Files\Merlin folder. To open the file, start up Excel (Start⇨Programs⇨Microsoft Excel). Then, since the spreadsheet is saved as a "csv" file, you must click on the ▼ for Files of Type: and select All Files (*.*). When you do this, the CompData file will appear in the dialog box. Click "Open" and the PerfData spreadsheet will open.

Exhibit 3.21

```
┌─────────────────────────────────────────┐
│ MTHS                                  ✕  │
├─────────────────────────────────────────┤
│                                          │
│    See File: C:\Program Files\Merlin\    │
│                 PerfData.csv             │
│                                          │
│              ┌──────────┐                │
│              │    OK    │                │
│              └──────────┘                │
└─────────────────────────────────────────┘
```

The contents of the PerfData spreadsheet are shown in Appendix I. Examining and plotting the variables in this spreadsheet will enable you to see trends in the performance of your and your competitors.

Select Quarter. The Select Quarter option allows you to change from the current quarter in which you are operating and select an earlier quarter of company operations. This will allow you to access earlier company reports and to view or print that information. The *Merlin* program retains all of your company's history on your company's disk. You will have the ability to view, and print, any or all of your company's reports from Quarter 1 through the current quarter of operation. However, this option will not allow you to return to an earlier quarter and change the decisions you made earlier.

To select a particular quarter, choose the Select Quarter option. Exhibit 3.22 shows the screen that will appear on your monitor. Enter the number of the quarter desired and select OK. If you select a quarter that has already been processed, none of the *decision* screens can be displayed since these decisions already have been made and cannot be changed. (However, you *can* see what decisions *were made* by examining the "Mkt. Product" or the "Mkt. Research Product" Reports.) If you select a quarter beyond the current quarter (e.g., Quarter 3 when you are making decisions for Quarter 2), you will receive an error message on the screen.

Exhibit 3.22

```
┌─────────────────────────────────────────┐
│                                          │
│         Enter the desired Quarter        │
│                                          │
│                 ┌───────┐                │
│                 │       │                │
│                 └───────┘                │
│                                          │
│   ┌──────────┐       ┌──────────┐        │
│   │    OK    │       │  Cancel  │        │
│   └──────────┘       └──────────┘        │
│                                          │
└─────────────────────────────────────────┘
```

Take note: When you process a quarter, you *must* use this option to view and/or print your results for the quarter that was just processed. The *Merlin* program automatically loads your company files for the next quarter of operation, *not for the quarter that has just been processed*. This means after Quarter 2 has been processed, Quarter 3 will appear on the screen when you load the *Merlin* program. To see the results of your Quarter 2 decisions and any market research information you have purchased, you have to choose the Select Quarter option and enter a "2" as the desired quarter number. You can then choose to view or print these results. Once you are ready to begin entering Quarter 3 decisions, choose the Select Quarter option again and enter a "3" as the quarter number.

Change Password. The first time you entered the *Merlin* program, you gave your company a password to prevent unwanted access to your company's reports that are stored on your disk. You may decide, for security reasons, to change your disk's password. This option allows you to make that change. You can change your password as often as you wish, but be careful. Frequent changes can lead to confusion. If you forget your password you will not be able to access the files on your disk, nor make decisions for the upcoming quarter of operation. If this happens, see your administrator for help.

To change your password, select the Change Password option. Exhibit 3.23 shows the screen that will appear on your monitor. Enter a new password you will remember and press [ENTER] or click on OK. Again, it is usually advisable not to select as a password the name of a family member or a nickname that others are likely to guess.

Exhibit 3.23

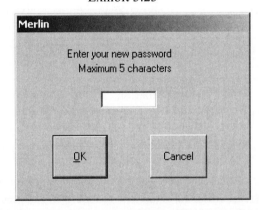

Change Company Name. As with the password, the first time you entered the *Merlin* program, you also gave your company a name that was saved onto your disk. As stated earlier, there is no relationship between your company name and the success or failure of your company. However, if you wish to change your company name at any time during the simulation exercise, use this option to do so. To do this, select the Change Company Name option. Exhibit 3.24 shows the screen that will appear on your monitor. Type in your new company name and press [ENTER] or click on OK.

Exhibit 3.24

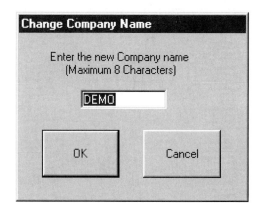

Save & Exit. This option saves your company's data file prior to exiting the *Merlin Team* or *Merlin Solo* program and returning you to Windows. ***It is extremely important that you save your decisions.*** If you are using a floppy disk and pull the disk from the drive without saving, everything you have done during your session will be ignored. Your decisions will revert to those that existed prior to the start of your session. You can enter decisions, request research, view your results, and print financial statements, but all of these actions will be lost if you pull your disk without saving your file.

If you started the *Merlin* program using your company disk, your decisions will be saved onto that disk. If you started the *Merlin* program using the hard drive, you will have to copy your company's data file from the hard drive to the company disk when you turn your decisions in to your administrator. Read how to do this under the "Using *Merlin* on a Hard Disk" section later in this chapter.

The Quarter Menu

The Quarter Menu is an alternative method from the Select Quarter option (described above) to change from one quarter of operation to a different quarter. As with the Select Quarter option, you can use this menu to access earlier company reports and to view or print out that information.

To use this method, select the Quarter menu option. A number of buttons with numbers will appear under the Quarter heading as is shown in Exhibit 3.25. Select the button number for the quarter you wish to view. There will only be buttons for the quarters that you are able to access. So if you are forecasting for Quarter 4, there will not be buttons for 5, 6, or higher. This is because those quarters have not yet been processed and consequently there are not yet reports to view for those quarters.

Exhibit 3.25

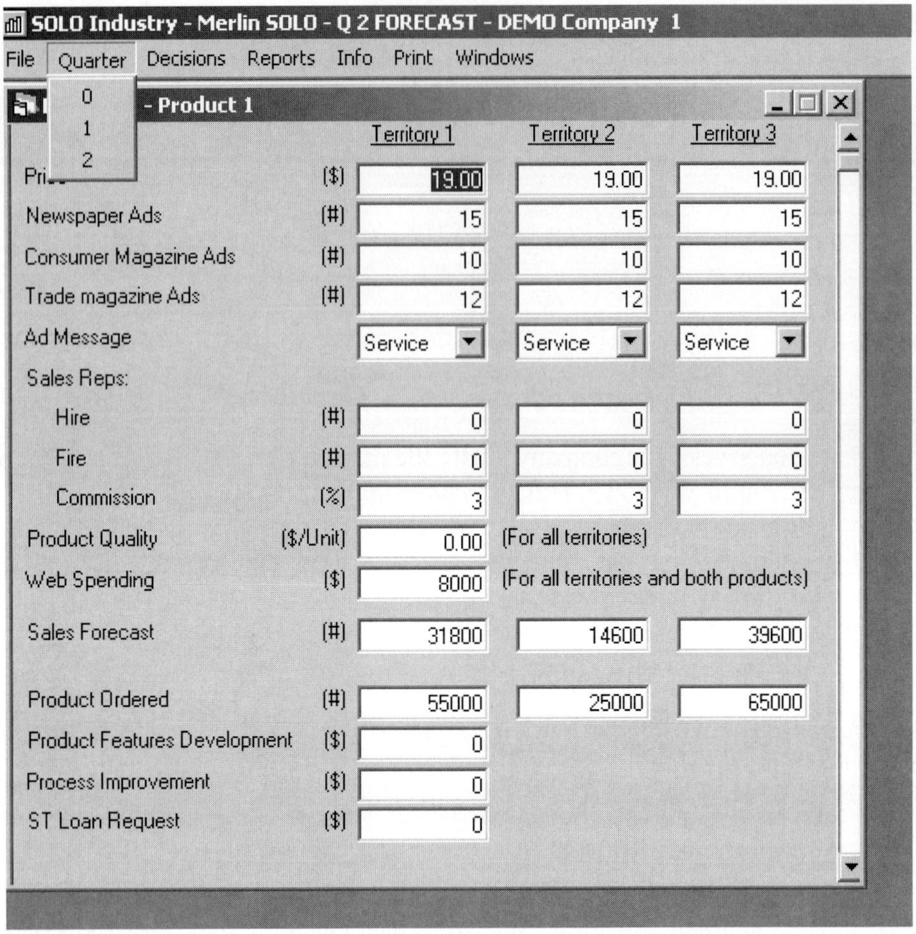

The Decisions Menu

The Decisions menu option provides you with access to the four screens on which you will enter your decisions for managing your company's operations (see Exhibit 3.26). Each of these will be discussed in order. Remember, you can access the decisions screens using either the Menu bar or *Merlin* "hot" keys. Press the F1 function key to move to the decisions screen for Product 1. Press F2 to move to the decisions screen for Product 2. Press F3 and F4 for the Marketing Research Decisions screens for Products 1 and 2, respectively.

Exhibit 3.26

🏢 SOLO Industry - Merlin SOLO - Q 2 FORECAST - DEMO Company 1				
File Quarter Decisions Reports Info Print Windows				

Mkt. Product 1	F1
Mkt. Product 2	F2
Mkt. Research Product 1	F3
Mkt. Research Product 2	F4

			Territory 2	Territory 3
Price		00	19.00	19.00
Newspaper Ads	(#)	15	15	15
Consumer Magazine Ads	(#)	10	10	10
Trade magazine Ads	(#)	12	12	12
Ad Message		Service ▼	Service ▼	Service ▼
Sales Reps:				
Hire	(#)	0	0	0
Fire	(#)	0	0	0
Commission	(%)	3	3	3
Product Quality	($/Unit)	0.00	(For all territories)	
Web Spending	($)	8000	(For all territories and both products)	
Sales Forecast	(#)	31800	14600	39600
Product Ordered	(#)	55000	25000	65000
Product Features Development	($)	0		
Process Improvement	($)	0		
ST Loan Request	($)	0		

Marketing. These screens allow you to enter your marketing decisions such as pricing, advertising and quality for the two products your company is marketing. You will also use this screen to enter your forecasts for the sales volume that you expect to achieve for each of your two products for the current quarter of operation. On the Decisions – Product 1 screen, you will also request the financing needed to pay for your marketing activities.

Marketing Research. These screens allow you to purchase market research about your competitors' marketing activities and the forecasted industry-wide demand for each of the products in future quarters. Each quarter, you will have the option of purchasing market research information for all your competitors or to designate up to three specific competitors on whom you wish to purchase the information you select.

The Reports Menu

The Reports menu allows you to access the reports detailing your company's operation. Exhibit 3.27 shows the reports that you can view using this option. When accessing these reports after loading *Merlin*, the program will display the reports for the most current quarter of operation. If you want to view an earlier quarter, you must first use either the Select Quarter option under the File menu heading or the Quarter menu, as were discussed earlier. We will discuss each of the reports used in *Merlin* in Chapter 7.

Exhibit 3.27

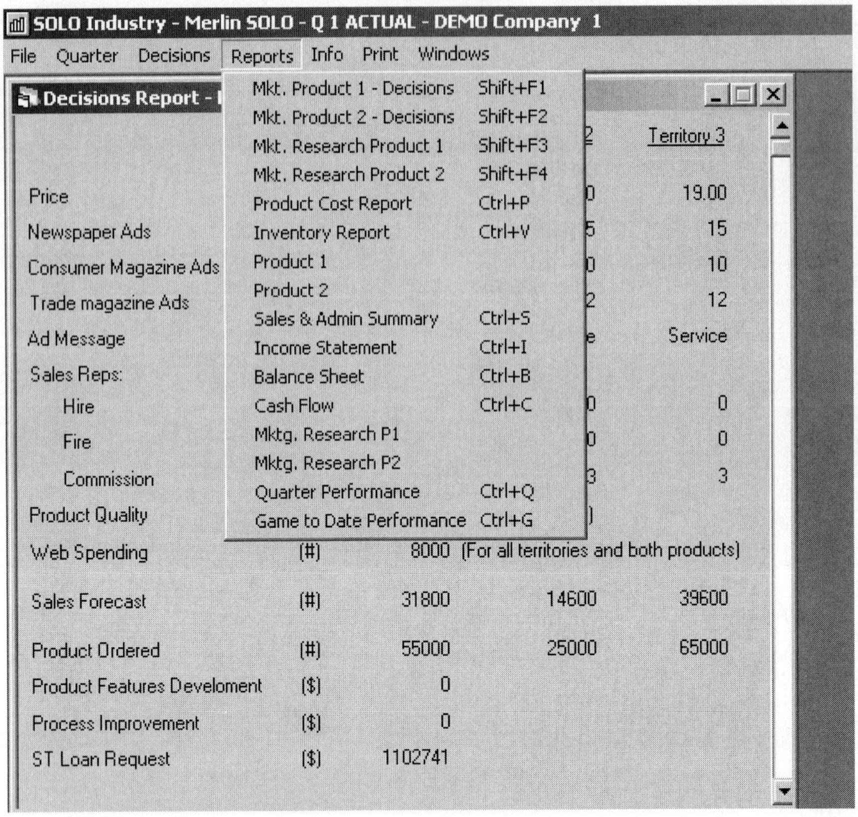

The Info Menu

The Info menu provides you with access to the costs involved in managing your *Merlin* company (see Exhibit 3.28). You can also access the Bulletin through the Info heading. We will discuss each of these options next.

Cost Parameters Report. Selecting this option will provide you with a listing of the costs for various items associated with operating your *Merlin* company. These include, for example, the costs for advertising, base cost of the products, features added to the products, and interest rates. You can also access the Cost Parameters screen using a "hot" key by pressing the F5 function key. The costs displayed on your monitor are the costs related to the quarter you are viewing. That is, if you are viewing Quarter 5, pressing F5 will show you the Cost Parameters screen for Quarter 5. These costs can change as you progress through the simulation. Therefore, you should check the cost report for the quarter for which you are making decisions to see if any changes have occurred. To view the costs for earlier quarters, use the Quarter menu option to choose the quarter you want to inspect. Then look at the cost report for that quarter. An example of a Cost Parameters Report is shown in Appendix E.

Bulletin. The Bulletin may have a message that your administrator wants to pass on to you. In *Merlin Team*, this message can change after your administrator processes company decisions. In *Merlin Solo*, this message can change after you submit your company data file to your administrator for review. So do not forget to check the bulletin after each time your administrator returns your *Merlin* data file to you. It is your responsibility to be aware of the information provided in the Bulletin. You can also access the Bulletin screen using the F6 "hot" key.

Exhibit 3.28

SOLO Industry – Merlin SOLO – Q 1 ACTUAL – DEMO Company 1				

File   Quarter   Decisions   Reports   Info   Print   Windows

Decisions Report – Product 1

| | | Cost Parameters F5 | | |
| | | Bulletin   F6 | | |

		Territory 1	Territory 2	Territory 3
Price	($)	19.00	19.00	19.00
Newspaper Ads	(#)	15	15	15
Consumer Magazine Ads	(#)	10	10	10
Trade magazine Ads	(#)	12	12	12
Ad Message		Service	Service	Service
Sales Reps:				
Hire	(#)	0	0	0
Fire	(#)	0	0	0
Commission	(%)	3	3	3
Product Quality	($/Unit)	0.00 (For all territories)		
Web Spending	(#)	8000 (For all territories and both products)		
Sales Forecast	(#)	31800	14600	39600
Product Ordered	(#)	55000	25000	65000
Product Features Develoment	($)	0		
Process Improvement	($)	0		
ST Loan Request	($)	1102741		

The Print Menu

The Print menu allows you to print any screen that appears on your monitor. You can choose to print an individual screen, a selection of screens, or all screens using this menu (see Exhibit 3.29). You can use this menu either (a) to print the screens you have selected to a printer connected to your computer or (b) to create a file containing the print image. We will explain how to do each of these next.

Exhibit 3.29

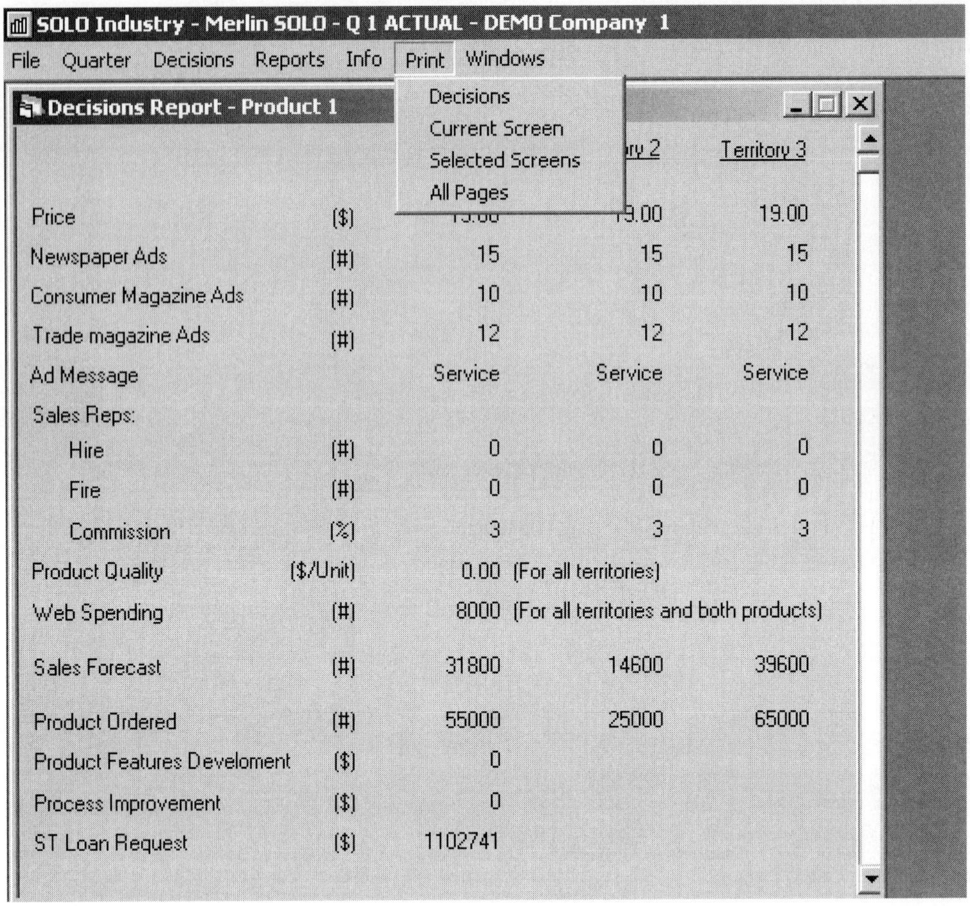

SOLO Industry - Merlin SOLO - Q 1 ACTUAL - DEMO Company 1					
File Quarter Decisions Reports Info **Print** Windows					
Decisions Report - Product 1					
			ry 2	Territory 3	
Price	($)	13.00	9.00	19.00	
Newspaper Ads	(#)	15	15	15	
Consumer Magazine Ads	(#)	10	10	10	
Trade magazine Ads	(#)	12	12	12	
Ad Message		Service	Service	Service	
Sales Reps:					
Hire	(#)	0	0	0	
Fire	(#)	0	0	0	
Commission	(%)	3	3	3	
Product Quality	($/Unit)	0.00 (For all territories)			
Web Spending	(#)	8000 (For all territories and both products)			
Sales Forecast	(#)	31800	14600	39600	
Product Ordered	(#)	55000	25000	65000	
Product Features Develoment	($)	0			
Process Improvement	($)	0			
ST Loan Request	($)	1102741			

Print menu dropdown items: Decisions / Current Screen / Selected Screens / All Pages

Print to a Printer. To print your selection of screens to a printer, select the screens you wish to print using one of the print options described below. After making your selection, a print dialogue box similar to that shown in Exhibit 3.30 will appear on your monitor. This dialogue box allows you to decide where you want to "print" the screens. If you want to send them to the printer connected to your computer, use the Tab key to move to the OK button and then press [ENTER] or use the mouse to select the OK button, to begin the printing of the screens.

Exhibit 3.30

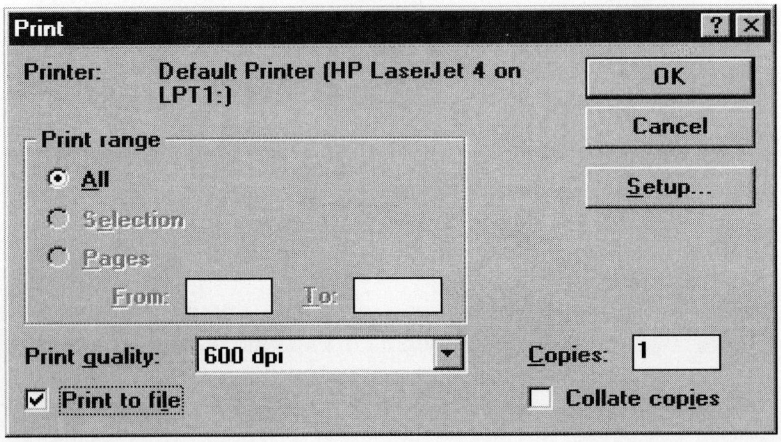

Print

Printer: Default Printer (HP LaserJet 4 on LPT1:)

Print range
- ⦿ All
- ○ Selection
- ○ Pages
  - From: ____   To: ____

Print quality: 600 dpi

☑ Print to file

OK   Cancel   Setup...

Copies: 1

☐ Collate copies

Print to a File. You also have the option of printing the screens to a file instead of a printer. You could then transfer the file electronically to a teammate at another location using a modem. If you want to select this option, use the mouse to "check" (✓) the Print to File option in the lower left corner of the dialogue box as is shown in Exhibit 3.30. Alternatively, you can use the Tab key to move the cursor to the box, then press the space bar to check the box. Then select the OK button.

Another dialogue box will appear on your monitor prompting you to name the file and select the location where you want to save the file (see Exhibit 3.31). A default file name will appear in the upper left corner. If you wish to change the file name, select a file name that describes the contents of the file. File names can be up to eight characters long. To store that file on your *Merlin Solo* company disk located in Drive A, select the "**a:**" drive option and press the Tab key to move to the OK button or use the mouse to click on OK.

Exhibit 3.31

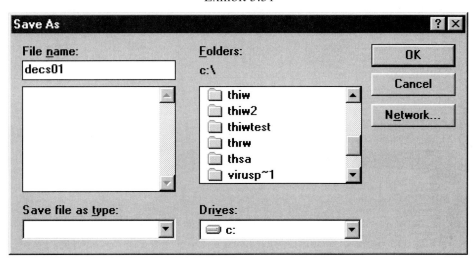

Print Decisions. Selecting this option will print the four decision screens: Decisions – Product 1, Decisions – Product 2, Marketing Research Decisions – Product 1, and Marketing Research Decisions – Product 2. To print these four screens, select the Print heading using the mouse or the Tab key, then select the Decisions option. Select the OK button to print the screens. To save the screens as a file, check (✓) the Print to File option box, then select the OK button and follow the directions given in the "Print to a File" section, above.

Print Current Screen. This option lets you print the last screen you were viewing before selecting this option. As with the Print Decisions option, a print dialogue screen will appear on your monitor so you can decide where you want to print the screen (see Exhibit 3.30). Select the OK button to print the screen. To save the screen as a file, check (✓) the Print to File option box, then select the OK button and follow the directions given in the "Print to a File" section, above.

Print Selected Screens. This option allows you to print only the report screens you desire. After selecting this option, a screen will appear with a listing of the reports you can choose to print (see Exhibit 3.32). Use the mouse to click on the report(s) you desire (e.g., the Income Statement) or use the Tab key to move to the screen you want printed and then press the space bar to select that screen. When you have selected all the screens desired, use the Tab key to move to the OK button and press [ENTER] or click on OK using the mouse. Select the OK button to print the screen. To save the screens as a file, check (✓) the Print to File option box, then select the OK button and follow the directions given in the "Print to a File" section, above.

Exhibit 3.32

Select Screens to Print
☐ Marketing Decisions P1   ☑ Income Statement
☐ Marketing Decisions P2   ☐ Balance Sheet
☐ Mkt. Research Decisions P1   ☐ Cash Flow Statement
☐ Mkt. Research Decisions P2   ☐ Cost Parameters
☑ Product Cost Report   ☐ Mkts. Research P1
☐ Inventory Reports   ☐ Mkts. Research P2
☐ Product 1 Report   ☑ Qtr. Performance Report
☐ Product 2 Report   ☐ Game Performance Report
☐ Selling/Admin Summary   ☐ Bulletin
OK   Cancel

All Pages. This option will automatically print all of the *Merlin Solo* screens. As with the Print Decisions option, a print dialogue screen will appear on your monitor so you can decide where you want to print the screens (see Exhibit 3.30). Select the OK button to print the screen. To save the screen as a file, check (✓) the Print to File option box, then select the OK button and follow the directions given in the "Print to a File" section, above.

SEEING THE *FORECASTED* RESULTS OF YOUR DECISIONS

Once you have entered decisions, you can view the *forecasted* reports for your company. These are not your "actual" results, like those that will exist after you have processed your decisions. Instead, these reports are based on the sales forecast that you entered on the decisions screens for Products 1 and 2. So, if you said, for example, that you would sell 36,000 units of Product 1 in Territory 1 at a price of $19.50 each, you will see in the forecasted Income Statement that you sold the 36,000 units and made $702,000 in sales on that product in that territory. However, when the *Merlin Solo* program actually processes your decisions, your sales may look very different! For example, if you sell only 30,000 units because of aggressive pricing by your competitors, your sales revenues for Product 1 in Territory 1 would be only $585,000. This reduction in sales revenues could move you from a profit to a loss for that quarter's operation. In other words, *your forecast reports are only as accurate as your sales forecasts*. If you are overly optimistic in your sales forecasts, your reports will reflect this optimism and may show profits that will be nonexistent after you process your company's decisions. The program will not warn you that your forecasts are inaccurate. It will only process your forecasts, not judge them. It is up to you to enter realistic sales forecasts. Chapter 6 discusses making a sales forecast in more detail.

You can view the reports to see what will be the effects of your decisions, *assuming that your sales forecast is accurate*. You can look through the reports using any one of the methods for moving around the screens that was described earlier. Notice that before you process your decisions, the reports are labeled as "Forecast" reports. After you process your *Merlin* decisions the reports will be labeled as "Actual" reports. The "Actual" reports are the ones that matter. These are the reports that will be used to determine your standing relative to your competition and that you will use to determine your decisions for your company's next quarter of operation.

PROCESSING THE DECISIONS (AVAILABLE ONLY FOR *MERLIN SOLO*).

After you have entered decisions, reviewed your anticipated performance by looking at forecasted results, and modified any decisions you wish, you are ready to process those decisions. We described the processing stage of working with *Merlin* in Chapter 1. Instructions for processing *Merlin Solo* are also provided earlier in this chapter. Processing the decisions will move you from the quarter in which you are now operating (e.g., Quarter 1) to the next quarter (e.g., Quarter 2).

SEEING THE _ACTUAL_ RESULTS OF QUARTERS THAT HAVE BEEN PROCESSED

As discussed earlier, when you load the *Merlin* program, it automatically advances to the next quarter for which you must make decisions. This means that if you want to view or print the actual (vs. forecasted) results for the quarters of your company's operations that have been processed, you will have to use the Select Quarter option under the File menu, or the Quarter menu, to index the program back to an earlier quarter. So, for example, after your decisions for Quarter 2 have been processed, your *Merlin* program will automatically set up for your company's Quarter 3 decisions. To see how your company performed in Quarter 2 and to see the market research information you purchased, select the Quarter menu and choose the "2" that drops down from the menu heading. You will then be able to view or print the actual results of your decisions and the market research information for Quarter 2. When you are ready to begin entering your Quarter 3 decisions, select the Quarter menu again and choose the "3" to return to the Quarter 3 screens. To view the actual results for Quarter 1, you would repeat this process choosing the "1" from the Quarter menu options.

DISPLAYING MULTIPLE SCREENS SIMULTANEOUSLY

Merlin is designed to allow you to display multiple screens on your monitor at the same time. This lets you enter decisions on one screen and simultaneously see the effect of that decision on one, or more, report screens. For example, Exhibit 3.33 shows that you can display all, or a portion, of the Decisions – P1, Income Statement, and Cash Flow screens at one time. In order to see more than one screen at a time, you will have to move them from where they are initially displayed on the monitor. To do this, open the screen with which you want to work (e.g., Income Statement). Next, position the mouse arrow (↖) in the title bar of that screen. Press and hold the left mouse button and drag the screen to the location on the monitor where you want to move it. Once you have the screen in the desired position, release the mouse button. This is standard Windows protocol for moving screens on a monitor. If you have questions on how to do this, consult a Windows manual for additional guidance.

As shown in Exhibit 3.33, you can have screens overlap each other. If you want to see the full screen of one that is partially covered, just click on any portion to the screen that is exposed and it will be displayed above all other screens showing on the monitor.

Exhibit 3.33

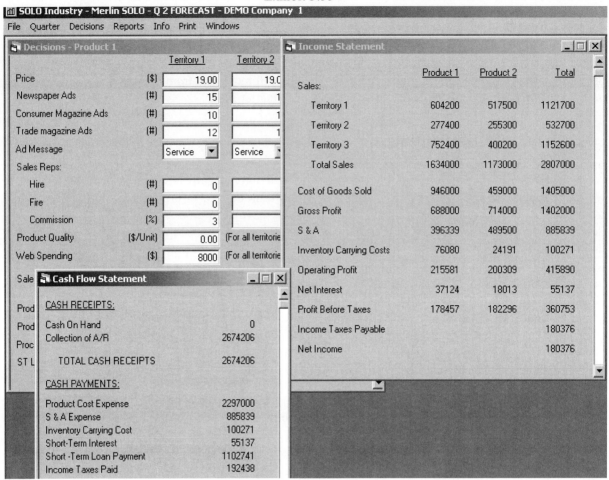

Simultaneously displaying multiple screens will help you to test quickly different decision entries. For example, you can change the price and forecasted sales volume, and see the effect on net income without having to leave the Marketing decisions screen and switch to the Income Statement screen. Using the multiple screen capabilities of the *Merlin* program allows you to fine-tune your decisions quickly and efficiently.

REPROCESSING A PREVIOUS QUARTER (APPLIES ONLY TO *MERLIN TEAM*)

This option is similar to the Start New Industry option for *Merlin Solo*, described earlier. But in *Merlin Team*, your administrator will decide when it will be used. This option is used only in very rare instances where it is necessary to make changes in decisions that have already been processed. If your administrator instructs you to repeat a previous quarter, use the Select Quarter option under the File menu heading. Enter the quarter number told to you by your administrator that is going to be re-processed. Next, select the Decisions menu heading. Notice that the "Change Decisions" option is now available. Exhibit 3.34 shows an example of what this screen looks like.

Exhibit 3.34

TeamDemo Industry	Merlin TEAM		Q 1 ACTUAL	COMPANY1 Company 1		
File Quarter Decisions Reports Info Print Windows						

Decisions						_ □ ×
	Mkt. Product 1		F1			
	Mkt. Product 2		F2			
	Mkt. Research Product 1		F3	y 1	Territory 2	Territory 3
	Mkt. Research Product 2		F4			
Price	Change Decisions			.00	19.00	19.00
Newspaper Ads		(#)		15	15	15
Consumer Magazine Ads		(#)		10	10	10
Trade magazine Ads		(#)		12	12	12
Ad Message				Service	Service	Service
Sales Reps:						
Hire		(#)		0	0	0
Fire		(#)		0	0	0
Commission		(%)		3	3	3
Product Quality	($/Unit)			0.00	(For all territories)	
Web Spending		(#)		8000	(For all territories and both products)	
Sales Forecast		(#)		31800	14600	39600
Product Ordered		(#)		55000	25000	65000
Product Features Develoment	($)			0		
Process Improvement		($)		0		
ST Loan Request		($)		1019459		

When you select the Change Decisions option, *Merlin Team* will ask for a password (see Exhibit 3.35). Enter the password your administrator has given you. You will then be able to enter new decisions for that quarter.

Exhibit 3.35

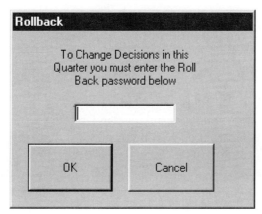

Rollback

To Change Decisions in this
Quarter you must enter the Roll
Back password below

[   ]

| OK | Cancel |

If you enter the wrong password, a dialogue box will appear on your monitor telling you that you entered the wrong password (see Exhibit 3.36). If you do not enter the correct password, you will not be allowed to enter decisions for that quarter.

Exhibit 3.36

Do not attempt to make changes on your own without the administrator's approval. Even if you succeed in doing so, the records your administrator keeps in the administrator's files will override your changes, put your company records in turmoil, and make successful completion of the simulation extremely difficult.

USING *MERLIN* ON A HARD DISK

As mentioned earlier in this chapter, you can work with *Merlin* using your computer's hard disk rather than on your company's floppy disk, if you so desire. If you use the hard disk, it is very likely that you will have to move files back and forth between the hard disk and a floppy.

Copying Files Between the Company Disk and the Hard Disk

If you plan to work with *Merlin* using your hard disk, you will need to use Windows Explorer to copy files. If you are unfamiliar with how to copy files using this Windows program, we strongly recommend that you do *not* use the hard disk to work with *Merlin*. We believe you would be much wiser to operate the *Merlin* program off of the company disk. The cost of copying an incorrect file to or from either the hard disk or the company disk is severe. The benefits do not outweigh the hazards involved. We suggest that you practice working with Windows Explorer in circumstances where mistakes are of less consequence.

If you choose to work off of your hard disk, use the following directions to copy the proper files to and from the hard disk and your company disk.

For *Merlin Team*.
- To copy files from the company disk to the hard disk: .
  Copy the MP.MTS file from your company disk in Drive A to the Program Files\Merlin directory created on your C Drive during your Windows setup.
- To copy files from the hard disk to the company disk:
  Copy the MP.MTS file from the Program Files\Merlin directory created on your C Drive during your Windows setup to your company disk in Drive A.

For *Merlin Solo*.
- To copy files from the company disk to the hard disk:
  Copy the company file that you created and saved when you started the simulation from your company disk in Drive A to the Program Files\Merlin directory created on your C Drive during your Windows setup.
- To copy files from the hard disk to the company disk:
  Copy your company file from the Program Files\Merlin directory created on your C Drive during your Windows setup to your company disk in Drive A.

  NOTE: The name of the file you must copy was established when you saved the file at the start of the simulation. The name of the file is the name you chose plus a ".MSS" extension. See the instructions and example for naming a company data file under "Starting the *Merlin Solo* Program". The file name used in the example was DEMO.MSS.

Make sure you do not accidentally forget to transfer your files from your hard disk to your *Merlin Solo* company disk before you submit the disk to your administrator. *You* are responsible for the accuracy of the decisions you turn in to your administrator, *not* the administrator! If you forget to transfer your files to your company disk, you will have to live with the consequences of this mistake, which could be severe. Just as in business, you have to be responsible for your mistakes.

MAKING A BACKUP DISK

You should always keep a backup of your *Merlin* company disk, or company data file if using the hard disk, to protect against unexpected damage or loss of your company's data. **It is your responsibility to protect your company's assets! This includes your *Merlin* data!** Just because you are careful does not mean nothing can, or will, go wrong. Bad luck does happen. It is up to you to protect against it.

Failure to maintain a backup of your company disk or company data file can have severe consequences. It is extremely important to make backups regularly. This will protect you in case your main disk is damaged in any way. Remember Murphy's Law: "If something can go wrong, it will, and usually at the worst time possible."

If Using a Company (Floppy) Disk. Make a backup copy of your *Merlin* company disk by using the Windows Explorer program. Click on My Computer and highlight the icon labeled "3½ floppy [A:]." Then select the Copy Disk option from under the File heading and follow the directions.

If Using the Hard Disk. If you are running *Merlin* using your hard disk, you need to copy your company data file (MP.MTS for *Merlin Team* or the name you chose when you started the simulation plus ".MSS" – see item 7, page 14 – for *Merlin Solo*) to a floppy disk for safekeeping. Make a backup of your company data file to a back up disk by following the directions for copying files from the hard drive to the company disk under the "Using the Hard Disk" section, above.

TROUBLESHOOTING

The *Merlin* program has undergone literally hundreds of hours of testing, both inside and outside the classroom. However, it is always wise for you to be prepared for "What do I do if...?" or "What do I do now?" situations.

Complete System Failure

The first thing to remember is that even if the computer system suddenly fails to operate (frequently referred to as a "crash"), the data on your *Merlin* company disk or on the hard disk will not be destroyed. In this worst-case scenario, restart the *Merlin* program. Any entries you had already saved will still be on your *Merlin* company disk or hard disk, depending on which you are using. If you have not yet saved your decisions, you will have to reenter them.

Merlin Program Failure

If the *Merlin* program file fails to load, the simplest response is to reload the *Merlin* program onto your hard disk using the CD in your manual. Before doing this, make sure you have current backup copies of your company data files. Reloading the *Merlin* program files will not change your company's current data file, but you should make copies to protect yourself in case the program failure is an indicator of problems with your computer's hard disk.

Merlin Company Disk Failure

Periodically, a sector of a disk becomes worn from high use or damaged by a disk drive as it reads from and writes to the disk. If the *Merlin* company disk fails to load because of disk damage, use your backup disk, if you have been keeping it up to date. If you have not maintained a backup disk, you will have to see your administrator to get your company data file restored.

Viruses

The danger of a virus contaminating your *Merlin* company data file on your company disk or hard disk and disabling the files stored on it is ever present. If your *Merlin* program will not operate, it may be the result of a virus infection. Run a virus check of your *Merlin* company disk and your hard disk to see if this has occurred. **If your company disk has a virus on it, do NOT try to use it in another machine without first removing the virus.** If you do not know how to do this, get help! Any continued use of the disk will only spread the virus to more computers.

It is your responsibility to keep your *Merlin* company disk free of viruses. You would be wise to scan your disk for viruses *every* time you use it and before anytime you turn it in to your administrator. Not doing this leaves you exposed to virus infections. Assume the worst whenever you use a computer that others have used.

Data Entry Errors

If you attempt to make data entries that are outside acceptable limits, you will receive an error message from the *Merlin* program. Press the [ESC] key to cancel the illegal entry and try again. Remember, you can change your entries as often as you like *before* they are processed. This is discussed in detail in Chapter 6 under the "Sales Forecast Estimate" heading.

A STEP-BY-STEP WALK-THROUGH

You should now be familiar with the mechanics of working with *Merlin*. Turn to Appendix K and follow its step-by-step directions. Use the *Merlin Solo* program and enter some decisions and look at the reports resulting from those decisions. Doing this will help you see how you can use the forecasting process to test decision options. It will also show you how your forecasted results will differ from your actual results. Then, go on to Chapter 6. We will discuss the decisions you have available to you to manage your *Merlin* company.

CHAPTER 4

THE *MERLIN* BUSINESS ENVIRONMENT

This chapter will provide you with a description of your *Merlin* company's business environment. It will also describe the beginning status of your company as well your company's products. In *Merlin Solo*, you will always manage Company 1.

You will manage your company over a number of decision rounds. Each decision round represents three months of operation (i.e., one quarter of a year). In the *Merlin* simulation, your operations begin in Quarter 1 (i.e., January – March). At the beginning of Quarter 1, all companies start from an identical position, explained in detail below.

YOUR COMPANY'S MARKETPLACE

For the duration of this simulation you will be selling your two products in three geographical territories. How much you sell in each territory will depend on the industry-wide demand for the products as well as how much effort you put into marketing your products compared to your competitors' efforts to sell their products. You must spend your money wisely and determine what mix of the marketing strategies will yield the best results. If your competitors do a better job of marketing their products, their market share will be better than yours.

To avoid distribution costs and to reflect market differences, your company has divided the market for your products into three sales territories, Territory 1, Territory 2, and Territory 3. There is quite a bit of diversity in the size and demographic composition of the three territories. A brief description of each of the territories follows.

Territory 1.   This territory is quite large, comprising approximately 40% of the total U.S. population and is also relatively affluent.

Territory 2.   Territory 2 is roughly half the size of Territory 1 (approximately 20% of the U.S. population) and has a similar demographic makeup. Consumers are typically relatively up-scale and generally open to new products.

Territory 3.   While similar in size to Territory 1 (about 40% of the U.S. population), the profile of the residents of Territory 3 is a bit different. These consumers have somewhat less disposable income and generally are less receptive to new products. Perhaps as a result of their lower incomes, the residents of Territory 3 have shown a tendency to be sharper bargain-hunters than are residents of the other two territories.

YOUR COMPANY

In the *Merlin* simulation you will manage a small company that was founded and operated by Emily, Erin, and Anne Scottlaw. The Scottlaws are entrepreneurs who establish and operate small businesses until they become commercially viable and then move on to new endeavors. After running this company for two years, the Scottlaws are ready for new challenges and have brought you in to take over the operation of the company.

As your term at the helm of your company begins, there will be from two to twelve companies in your industry (including yours). All of the companies share exactly the same position — identical products, equal market share, same financial condition, etc. at the beginning of Quarter 1. The decisions that you make will determine how your company will fare in the years ahead, so it is important that your mission and strategies enable you to compete effectively.

Your company sells two products, Product 1 and Product 2. While your company does not actually manufacture the products — rather, you contract production to a supplier — you do maintain a staff of technical specialists who work closely with the supplier to design and set specifications for the products you sell. Each quarter (every three months) you must decide how many units of each of the two products you will order from the supplier.

You sell your two products to retailers who, in turn, sell them to the ultimate consumers. The prices you charge for your products, the level of quality you build into them, plus how you choose to promote them, are decisions you will constantly face.

YOUR PRODUCTS

As stated above, all *Merlin* companies compete against each other for customers to sell two products — Product 1 and Product 2. We have purposely not identified these two products. Your instructor may choose to have each product represent a particular product, or to leave them generic in nature. In either case, one of your objectives will be to determine what influence the various elements of the marketing mix have on the consumers' decision to buy either product in the *Merlin* environment.

You will sell these products through retailers to the general public. The two products are not substitutes for one another, nor are they complementary. This means that sales of one product do not affect sales of the other product. You should not count too heavily on customers buying your product simply because of past experiences with either of your products. While there is likely to be some brand loyalty, your company is too new to the market to expect brand satisfaction with one of your products to boost the sales of your other product.

Although each company in *Merlin* begins the simulation selling identical products, the amount you spend on quality and the investment you make in product features can create differences in future periods. Of course, the magnitude of the differences will depend on how your expenditures compare to those of your competitors. If you and your competitors all spend similar amounts, the customers may recognize that you have a high-quality product, but see it as no different from your competitors' high-quality product. In other words, how much you invest in quality on a *relative* basis is as important as how much you spend on an absolute basis.

The following paragraphs present a brief description of the two products.

Product 1:

Product 1 is a rather basic product. While the Scottlaws began marketing this product only two years ago, the product category has been around for several years. Consumers are quite familiar with the product and how it's used. Prices and profit margins have slipped a bit since the Scottlaws began selling the product. In Quarter 0 your company sold this product to retailers for $19.00; the production cost was $11.00. The total cost includes the sub-contractor's manufacturing costs plus the costs to distribute the product to retailers for sale to the ultimate consumer. Consumers do not have strong brand preferences for this product, nor do they put much effort into comparing options before making their purchase decision for Product 1.

Product 2:

Although Product 2 costs only $27 to produce and deliver, the Scottlaws sold it to retailers for $69 in Quarter 0. Many consumers are unfamiliar with the Product 2, because it was just recently introduced to the market. Unfortunately, all companies in your industry had been working simultaneously on its development, so all your competitors brought out their products at about the same time as you did. Because the product is new, most customers seriously consider the elements of the product offer (features, price, quality, etc.) before making their purchase decision. Some retailers have been reluctant to carry Product 2 because of its limited sales volume.

DEMAND FOR YOUR PRODUCTS

While the demand for your products is not entirely predictable, you can purchase demand estimates for future quarters. These demand estimates can be extremely valuable in helping you determine appropriate order quantities, deciding which of your products deserves more resources, etc. Starting with Quarter 1, you can purchase future demand estimates simply by requesting these estimates on the Marketing Research decision forms. Quarter 1 is the only quarter for which you are unable to buy demand estimates. Because you cannot purchase information for Quarter 1, we provide those demand estimates here.

Unless your simulation administrator informs you otherwise, the demand estimates for Quarter 1 are:

Product 1

Territory 1	Territory 2	Territory 3
31800	14600	39600

Product 2

Territory 1	Territory 2	Territory 3
7500	3700	5800

The demand estimates you see above represent the *average number* of units that will be sold by a *single company* in your industry. Thus, the 31,800 figure is an estimate of the number of units of Product 1 that an *average firm* will sell in Territory 1 in the first Quarter. **In all future periods, the demand estimates represent the *total number* of units that will be sold in your entire industry.** [So, if there are twelve firms competing in your industry, the estimate of total industry demand for Product 1, Territory 1, Quarter 1 is 381,600 units (31,800 x 12)]. Since we cannot know how many companies will be competing in your industry, we cannot provide an estimate of total demand for Quarter 1.

SUBSTITUTE PRODUCTS

While there are no *direct* substitutes for the products sold by your industry, there are products that are similar. As a result, the total size of your industry's market is influenced by the actions of the competitors in your industry. If the marketing efforts of the firms in your industry are exceptionally aggressive, the total sales for your industry will expand as sales are won from producers of these substitute products. On the other hand, if the promotional efforts of all companies in your industry are very passive, customers will stop buying this type of product and will begin buying substitute goods from companies outside your industry. Total industry demand will suffer. In the *Merlin* environment, a weak marketing effort may be disastrous. Not only will one company suffer, but the whole industry may decline.

The next chapter will give a review of the fundamentals of the marketing management process and show how that process relates to this simulation. Then, Chapter 6 will explain the decisions you will have to make each quarter as you manage your *Merlin* business.

CHAPTER 5

REVIEW OF MARKETING MANAGEMENT FUNCTIONS

The purpose of this chapter is to review the marketing management process. This review is not meant to replace a traditional textbook on marketing. Exhibit 5.1 provides a flow chart of the typical sequence of activities involved in the process of marketing management.

Exhibit 5.1
The Strategic Marketing Management Process

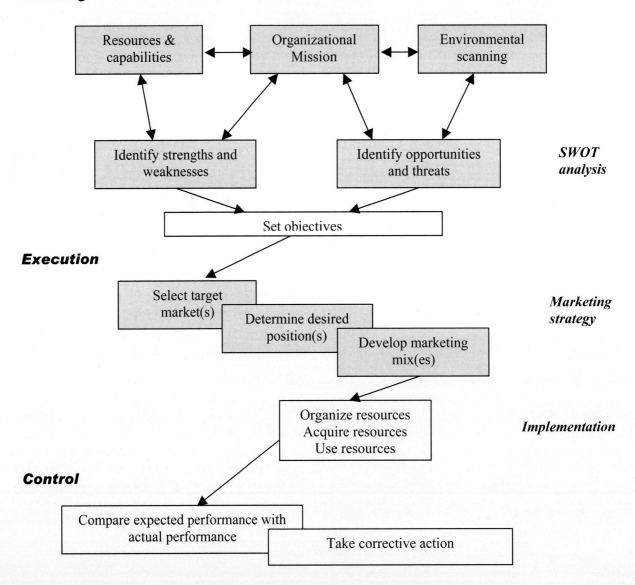

Planning

Resources & capabilities ⟷ Organizational Mission ⟷ Environmental scanning

Identify strengths and weaknesses   Identify opportunities and threats   *SWOT analysis*

Set objectives

Execution

Select target market(s)   *Marketing strategy*

Determine desired position(s)

Develop marketing mix(es)

Organize resources
Acquire resources
Use resources   *Implementation*

Control

Compare expected performance with actual performance   Take corrective action

The aim of marketing planning is to secure a
sustainable competitive advantage for the organization.

MISSION STATEMENT

Planning usually starts with a specific statement of the mission and objectives of the firm. The mission statement describes the purpose of the organization. It states what business your company wants to be in. Mission statements are designed to provide a stable direction for the organization, so they should be broad and general enough to withstand considerable changes in the marketplace. Mission statements should be revised only infrequently. Mission statements take into account both the essential *internal* and *external* environments of your organization.

A good mission will capitalize on the strengths and capabilities of the organization. Before writing the statement, you should have a thorough understanding of what it is that sets your organization apart from that of your competitors. What resources or capabilities does your organization possess that your competitors can't easily match? What is it that your organization is uniquely qualified to do? Of all activities that your organization might engage in, what are you best at?

An organization's mission should be broad enough to provide the latitude to adapt to changing conditions (i.e., to avoid what Theodore Leavitt refers to as marketing myopia). Yet, it must provide the focus necessary to keep your company from drifting into activities for which it is poorly suited. It should be written with an eye to the future. You should understand and attempt to anticipate likely changes in the external environments within which your firm operates. To accomplish this task, you must have an effective information gathering function. Mission statements should not be set in isolation.

SWOT ANALYSIS

An examination of the internal and external environments of the organization and a statement of the corporate mission flows into SWOT (Strengths, Weaknesses, Opportunities, and Threats) analysis. The internal components — your organization's resources and capabilities – should lead to identifying your firm's strengths and weaknesses, while the external components (gleaned through environmental scanning) should lead to identifying your firm's opportunities and threats. As you perform the SWOT analysis, you might decide that you should revise your mission statement to take better advantage of your firm's competitive position.

OBJECTIVES

Within the general framework of the mission, your company should set explicit objectives – specific goals you will strive to achieve. Almost all organizations have multiple objectives – profit and volume objectives are almost universal, with many firms also stating objectives relating to resource utilization and efficiency. For example, you might set a profit objective of achieving a 5% net return on sales (i.e., ROS). A volume objective could be to maintain a 15% market share in Territory 1. Examples of resource utilization and efficiency objectives could include being granted an emergency loan on no more than one occasion per eight quarters; or to average no more than one stockout for the six product-territory combinations per quarter.

Your mission statement will often have obvious implications for your objectives. If you intend to be an ultra-high quality producer serving the most affluent customers, it is unlikely that you will be able to achieve a high market share. The position occupied by your organization will also influence your objectives. It is, of course, imperative that your objectives reflect your organization's strengths and weaknesses as well as the opportunities and threats facing your firm. Without a solid understanding of your organization's mission and internal and external environments, it is virtually impossible to formulate appropriate objectives.

While the corporate mission should be broad and long-lived to provide stability for the organization, the objectives must be updated periodically. It is generally accepted that objectives should meet the criteria described in Exhibit 5.2. In addition, if you have more than one objective, you must take into account the relationship among the objectives. A good set of objectives will avoid putting the organization in a position where accomplishing one objective has negative consequences for another objective. For example, the previously stated example of a 15% market share in Territory 1 is easily measurable. If the company is competing in *Merlin Solo* the objective is also challenging since the industry consists of 12 companies. That means, if sales were equally divided among the 12 companies, each company would have an 8% market share (i.e., 1/12). In fact, you might argue that the 15% target is not realistic, since it involves achieving nearly double your fair share of the market of 8%. You might also question whether a company could achieve a 15% market share and still maintain the 5% net ROS target. If not, the volume objective is inconsistent with the profit objective.

Sometimes the shorter-term objectives of a firm will differ from their longer-term goals. For example, a company may sacrifice some profits in the short term and attempt to build market share in the hopes of achieving a market position that will permit earning above average profits in the long run. An illustration of this approach would be a company that greatly increased its advertising in the short term in the belief that the increased visibility would create a superior market position and increased profits in the longer run. There are constraints on the freedom to set objectives, however. In our economy, virtually no company can afford to disregard profits for too long.

Exhibit 5.2

CHARACTERISTICS OF GOOD OBJECTIVES

Objectives should be:

1.	**Measurable**.	They should be both **Quantitative** and **Specific**. Each objective should have a definite, stated time frame. An objective should be measurable and sufficiently specific so that after the stated time period has passed, it should be clear whether or not the objective was achieved.
2.	**Challenging**.	Good objectives should demand that the organization strive to reach its potential.
3.	**Attainable/Realistic**.	While good objectives should be challenging, they should *not* be impossible.
4.	**Consistent**.	Objectives should be mutually achievable. Objectives should also be consistent with the strategies and tactics to be used for their accomplishment. (See Exhibit 5.4, Tests of Consistency of Objectives and Strategies for additional criteria.)

STRATEGY FORMULATION

Your objectives make an explicit statement of where you want to go. Now you must develop a plan for getting to your destination. Your marketing strategy is your general blueprint for accomplishing your goals. Strategy can be distinguished from tactics; tactics are concerned with the immediate, specific actions that are required to carry out a strategy. Strategy is the general plan that you will follow. For example, while your strategy may be to be that of a low-cost, low-price operator, you must decide how much money you will spend on process improvements to drive your costs down and what price you will charge for each of your products in each territory.

Marketing strategy consists of three components – (1) selecting a target market (or markets); (2) determining a desired position; and (3) developing an appropriate marketing mix. In selecting a target market, you must ask whether there are different segments that are likely to react differently to variations in the marketing mix. Some firms view the marketplace as having no distinguishable segments leading them to pursue an undifferentiated marketing strategy – that is, they develop a single marketing mix designed to appeal to the entire market. Other firms see the marketplace as consisting of distinct segments of customers. They may elect to develop a single marketing mix to sell to a specific segment of the market or they may produce multiple marketing mixes each designed to appeal to a different market segment. In *Merlin* you might segment the market geographically with each territory a distinct segment, or you might attempt to appeal to the quality-conscious segment of the market.

Once a firm has decided to target a specific segment (or segments), it must decide what position will be most attractive to that segment. If the segment is motivated by ease of use, you would want to be perceived as the most convenient product on the market. The most effective strategy is usually related to those characteristics that are valued most highly by the customers in your target market. However, you must be careful not to ignore competition in the selection of a position. If all competitors are pursuing the same market segment or are attempting to achieve the same position, you may be more effective in selecting an alternative segment or position. For example, if all your competitors are vying to be the high price, high-quality supplier, you may realize better results if you position your product as an inexpensive alternative than if you elect to be yet another high price, high-quality supplier.

The final element of the marketing strategy consists of selecting an appropriate marketing mix. The way in which you manipulate the 4 Ps — the configuration of your product offering, the price you charge, the way that you promote your product, and the distribution (place) of the product — should all be consistent with the target market you have selected and the position you hope to achieve. Marketing theory provides considerable information on factors that influence how the market will respond to changes in the marketing mix. When setting your strategies, give careful consideration to such things as the nature of your products (convenience product, shopping product, etc.) and the stage of the product life cycle. An objective of building market share requires a very different strategy for a convenience product than for a heterogeneous shopping product. Similarly, the nature of the market must be taken into account. Some target markets may be highly responsive to price while other markets may be affected more by other elements of the marketing mix. Effective formulation of the 4 Ps is unlikely without a solid understanding and application of marketing theory. In *Merlin*, you will have the ability to determine your product's configuration (i.e., its level of quality and the number of features), its price, how you promote it (e.g., trade magazine ads versus sales representatives versus web-based promotions), and the place (i.e., territory) where you will promote it. Make sure you are consistent in the application of the 4 Ps of marketing as you manage your company.

A particularly important component of promotional strategy involves the selection of a "pull" versus a "push" strategy. It is important to choose the strategy that is consistent with your product. A push strategy involves promoting a product to channel members hoping that they, in turn, will promote the product to the next member in the channel. For example, a producer may advertise in trade magazines, send sales representatives to retailers to promote her products, and/or offer various incentives to the retailer. The producer does this in the hope that the retailer will place a high value on the product and choose to promote it to the ultimate consumer. In contrast, a pull strategy uses heavy promotion by the producer directed toward the ultimate customer in an attempt to draw the product through the channel. For example, a producer may use promotional tools (usually consumer advertising) to generate consumer demand for her product. In this case, if the consumers create a sufficient demand at the retail level, the retailers generally will want to carry the product. Exhibit 5.3 illustrates the difference between a push and pull strategy.

Exhibit 5.3

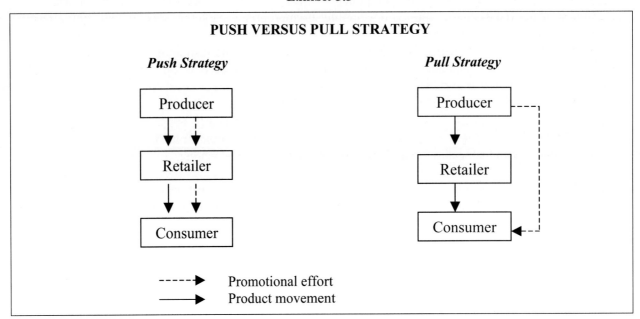

In practice, most marketers use a combination of push and pull, but the emphasis placed on the alternative strategies is likely to vary depending on market conditions and the nature of the product. (Almost all marketing texts discuss this topic. See, for example, Kotler and Armstrong, *Principles of Marketing*, 8th edition, p. 435.) Again, marketing theory can serve as a useful guide to your strategy development.

Once you have formulated your marketing strategy, you should ask yourself the following question: If we follow this strategy does it seem likely that we will achieve our objectives? It is imperative that the strategy you select is consistent with the objectives you set. Exhibit 5.4 provides a set of criteria for evaluating your goals and strategies.

Exhibit 5.4

TESTS OF CONSISTENCY OF OBJECTIVES AND STRATEGIES

- **Internal Consistency**
    - Are the goals mutually achievable?
    - Do the strategies address the goals?
    - Do the strategies reinforce each other?

- **Environmental Fit**
    - Do the goals and strategies exploit industry opportunities?
    - Do the goals and strategies deal with industry threats to the degree possible with available resources?
    - Are the goals and strategies responsive to broader societal concerns?

- **Resource Fit**
    - Do the goals and strategies match the resources available to the company relative to competitors?
    - Does the timing of the goals and strategies reflect the organization's ability to change?

- **Communication and Implementation**
    - Are the goals well understood by the key implementers?
    - Is there a close enough match between the goals and strategies and the values of the key implementers to insure commitment?
    - Is there sufficient managerial capability to allow for effective implementation?

- These questions are taken from Michael E. Porter's modification of criteria presented in K. R. Andrews, *The Concept of Corporate Strategy*, New York: Dow Jones-Irwin, 1971.

EXECUTING THE STRATEGY

Your marketing strategy provides a description of the general path you will follow in an attempt to achieve your objectives. However, to implement your strategy, you must make the specific decisions and carry out actions that will put that strategy into effect. For example, you may have planned a strategy to be a low price, minimal service operator, but you still must decide what specific price will you set for your product today. These specific tactical decisions are required to implement your strategy. Failure to implement good tactical decisions will lead to poor results regardless of how well you designed your strategy.

Strategy execution involves marshalling the necessary resources and using them efficiently. No company has unlimited resources. Effective managers must optimize the use of the resources they have. The starting point for much business planning is the sales forecast. From production scheduling to promotional expenditures, forecasts drive much of the planning of an organization. It will be up to you as you manage your company to determine what volume of sales you wish to achieve. Of course, just because you set a sales target, does **_not_** guarantee that you will achieve it.

The marketplace is dynamic and unpredictable. Whatever action you take is sure to result in counteractions from your competitors. In an environment this complex, how can a manager make wise decisions? On-the-job experience is, of course, a valuable asset. Research can also be extremely helpful. Obtaining information can be time-consuming and expensive, so gathering unnecessary information is worse than useless. However, making decisions in a vacuum is foolhardy. One of the keys to successful management is determining what information can be useful, placing an appropriate value on that information, gathering that needed information, *and* using it effectively.

Knowing how a market generally responds to marketing variables can be invaluable. The effectiveness of most marketing variables tends to follow an "s-curve". Small expenditures on any marketing variable are likely to generate little response; a critical threshold must be crossed. Once you cross that threshold, you are likely to see increasing response for additional marketing expenditures. However, at some point the marketer is likely to see diminishing returns; additional expenditures are likely to generate less and less response until we reach a point where additional expenditures are a waste of money. While marketers are aware of the general shape of the sales-response function, it is never easy to determine exactly where we are on the s-curve at any given time.

Exhibit 5.5

The Sales-Response Function
(The "S-Curve")

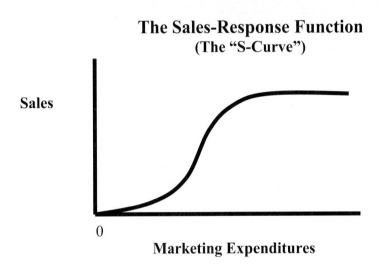

Sales

0

Marketing Expenditures

CONTROLLING THE MARKETING PROCESS

The work of the marketing manager is never done. Once you have made and executed your decisions, the market place responds. As a manager, you receive feedback primarily in the form of financial reports. Rarely will everything transpire exactly as you hope. It is your responsibility to evaluate the performance of your organization and to adjust your decisions accordingly. The marketplace never stands still — consumer tastes changes, competitors make moves and countermoves, and laws and regulations evolve. Operating an on-going concern requires constant supervision and alterations of tactics. The ability to interpret financial statements, production reports, marketing research, etc., is a critical component of the marketing manager's job.

CHAPTER 6

MAKING DECISIONS

OVERVIEW OF DECISIONS

This chapter will discuss the content of the decisions, not the process for entering them. Since this simulation emphasizes the marketing functions of the business, most of the decisions that you will need to make and enter concern elements of the marketing mix. You must make decisions for:
- Product
- Price
- Promotion

Your channels of distribution are fixed for the duration of the simulation – you will sell your products to retailers. In addition to these marketing decisions, as operators of a small business, you must make several decisions that support your marketing operations.
- Marketing research
- Sales forecasting
- Process cost reduction
- Product ordered
- Short term loan

These decisions are entered on the decision screens that you previewed in Chapter 3. In this chapter we will describe each of the decisions you will make. Refer to Chapter 3 if you are uncertain how to use the software to enter the decisions on the screens.

THE MARKETING PLAN

In *Merlin Solo* you compete in an established industry consisting of your company plus eleven competitors. In *Merlin Team*, the simulation administrator will inform you of the number of competitors. As stated in Chapter 4, you are taking over the leadership of a company that was started two years earlier. *All firms in your industry start this simulation in an identical position.*

Before you make any decisions, you should develop a marketing plan for your company. This is an important first step to help you cohesively tie together all your decisions. Without an explicit plan, various parts of your business could be working against each other. For example, you might wish to sell a high volume, but fail to allocate the necessary promotional expenditures to accomplish the task. If you order more units than you can sell, you will end up with excess inventory and be forced to pay carrying costs. Developing a business plan can help you avoid working toward conflicting goals.

Developing a Marketing Plan

Chapter 5 discussed the steps in the marketing management process – creating a mission statement, writing objectives, and developing strategies. The first step of the planning process is to develop a mission statement for your company because the mission statement should drive many of your decisions.

Consider two very different company missions. One would be to meet the needs of affluent (relatively price-insensitive) customers seeking a high quality product. For these customers, quality, not price, is the primary determinant of their decision-making process. The opposite focus would be to meet the needs of customers who are less concerned about the quality of the product and choose to budget much less for the purchase. This does not mean that quality is unimportant, but that it is a secondary issue after price.

These two different company missions would result in two very different strategies. Regardless of which strategy you pursue, you will face the same set of decisions involving product, price, and promotion. However, different missions will necessitate very different implementation. The high-quality focus would lead to a differentiation strategy, placing emphasis on quality and features. The low price focus would lead to a low-cost strategy resulting in efforts to lower the company's process costs so that you can earn a profit even at a low price. Reread Chapter 5 to guide you in the development of your company's marketing plan. Once you make this plan and set your overall strategies, you are ready to begin making the specific decisions described in this chapter.

We will now discuss in detail the situation facing your firm in *Merlin* and the decisions you will make each quarter.

MARKETING DECISIONS

For each quarter, you will have a number of marketing decisions to make. These include:
- Product
  - Quality
  - Features
- Price (i.e., setting prices for both of your products in each of the three sales territories)
- Promotion
  - Sales force (i.e., determining the number of salespeople and amount of sales commission for each product in each territory)
  - Media (i.e., selecting the number of newspaper ads, consumer magazine ads, trade magazine ads, and web spending)
  - Advertising message (i.e., deciding whether to emphasize price, features, quality, service or benefits)

In addition to these marketing decisions, you may choose to purchase demand estimates and other marketing research information. Combining the demand estimate information with your own marketing efforts and your expectations of your competitors' marketing efforts, you can estimate how many units of each product you will sell. Your sales estimates will help to determine how many units of each product you should order from your supplier.

Another decision that you must make each quarter is whether you wish to spend money in an attempt to achieve process improvements. While process improvements will not influence the number of units you sell, they will affect your profitability. Process improvements decrease the cost of production, thus improving your profit margins.

Finally, by comparing your expenditures and your estimated revenues, you must decide whether you wish to take a short-term loan.

You will enter each of your decisions for Product 1 and Product 2 and order marketing research information (including sales forecasts). We will now discuss each of these decisions in greater detail.

Product

The Scottlaws have informed you that you will not be able to develop any new products during the time that you will manage the company. If you wish, you may discontinue selling either product (or both products) in one or more territories. *To drop a product in one or more territories, simply discontinue all promotional spending for the product and enter the maximum allowable price ($49.99 for Product 1 and $149.99 for Product 2).*

Features. You may choose to add *features* to either or both of your products by spending money on research and development (R&D). There are two costs associated with adding a feature:

1. Feature development cost. As is virtually always the case with product development this is an uncertain endeavor. You can engage your technical specialists to work with the supplier to develop new features, but it is unclear how much time and money it will take before you actually succeed in adding a feature to the product. You do know that the more you spend, the more likely it is that a feature will be added and that your expenditures are cumulative – that is, if you don't spend enough to obtain a feature in this period, your money is not lost. Spending more dollars the next period may result in an additional feature being added to the product. You can elect to spend from $0 to $99,999 per quarter for feature development for Product 1 or Product 2.

2. Increased manufacturing cost. Every feature added to a product increases the cost of producing a unit of that product. Unlike the development cost which is an "up-front cost", the increased *production* cost applies to each unit you sell. The Cost Parameters Screen displays the per unit cost of each added feature for Product 1 and Product 2. The entire amount of the per-unit cost increase will be passed on to you. Once a feature has been added to a product, it is added to that product in all territories. You cannot eliminate a feature once you have added it to the product.

You can tell whether you were successful in adding a feature by looking at the very last line of the Sales and Administration Summary. It displays the total number of features that have been incorporated into each of your products. You will also see a change in the Features Costs line on the Product Cost Report Screen.

Quality. Another decision that you must make with respect to the product is the *quality* level that you will establish for each of your products. By choosing to spend money on quality, you may succeed in improving the quality of your products. Quality refers to durability, reliability, and freedom from defects of your products. There is no upfront investment required to improve quality, but there is a per-unit cost you can make. The more money you spend on quality, the more it increases the quality of your product, but it isn't clear *how much* of a sales increase will result from this spending. In addition, consumers judge the quality of your product relative to that of competing products. As a result, consumer perception of the quality of your product depends, not only on the quality of your product, but also on the quality of your competitors' products. You can spend anywhere from $0 to $99 per unit for Product 1 or Product 2 in any quarter. Note that customer perception of the quality of your products will be based on the quality investment *per unit*, not on the total amount spent.

Price

Each quarter you must make six price decisions; you must set the price for both products in each of the three regions. These prices will be the amount that you charge the retailers who sell your products in each area. Prices can differ between territories and, of course, from quarter to quarter. Wild fluctuations in price tend to confuse consumers and result in lost customers.

The Effect of Price on Sales. The price of your product affects sales in two ways; how your price compares to your competitors' prices and how your price has changed from last quarter to the current quarter. The price you charge compared to your competitors' prices has the biggest effect on your sales. Considering price alone, a product priced at $70 will sell more than one priced at $71. In addition, a *change* in price from last quarter also has an effect on how much you will sell. All other things being equal, if you just raised your price, you will sell less than if you had kept price constant from one quarter to the next. If you just lowered your price, you will sell more. The bigger the change in price, the greater the effect that price change will have on demand.

Setting Prices. To determine the price you will charge for a product, you need to consider:
    (a) The product's value offered to customers that is created by its combination of price and quality;
    (b) The cost of manufacturing your product;
    (c) The profit margin you desire for each product; and
    (d) The competitiveness of your prices relative to those of rival firms.

This means that you have to consider what it will cost to purchase those units from your subcontractor. In addition to the cost of purchasing products from your supplier, you should include a sufficient markup to cover other operating costs and provide a reasonable profit for your company. If you do not do this, you will be unable to continue in business over the long term. These costs include your marketing expenses as well as the costs of operating your business. The marketing and administrative costs are shown on the Sales and Administration Summary report that is explained in detail in Chapter 7. Inventory carrying costs and the finance charge for loans are shown on your Income Statement.

> NOTE: You can determine your cost for each unit of Product 1 or Product 2 by viewing the Product Cost Report. It shows your total product cost (which is your base cost less any process improvements, plus any additional costs for quality and features).

While it is important to set your price sufficiently high, you cannot price your product in isolation. You will have to adjust your price to meet the competitive moves of other companies in your industry. In the short run you may find that, to remain competitive, you may have to price your products at a level that will not cover all the costs of operating your business. Beware, however, that a short-term competitive pricing move does not lead you into a permanent unprofitable pricing strategy. Failure to develop a long-term company strategy that yields reasonable profits will result in the ruin of your business.

Promotion

You must make a number of decisions regarding the way in which you will promote your products. Note that the costs for the various forms of promotion described below are shown on the Cost Parameters screen. You can access this screen under the Info heading on the Menu bar, or by simply pressing the F5 hot key.

The impact of your promotional efforts is affected by (a) how much you promote your products and (b) how much you promote them relative to your competitors. You will need to think carefully about how much you wish to spend on promotion. If you spend too much promoting your products, your profits will be affected adversely. Purchasing, say four pages of newspaper advertising for Product 1 at $3,500 each, adds $14,000 to your costs. If your price for Product 1 is $19.00 and the cost of purchasing each unit from your supplier is $11.00, you earn $8.00 for every unit you sell. Your advertising will need to increase sales by 1,750 units (1,750 units x $8 = $14,000) just to cover the cost of your advertising.

At the same time, however, you will have to promote each of your products to achieve visibility in the marketplace. If you do not promote your products at all, or only minimally, potential customers will not be aware of your products' value relative to that of your competitors. Your chances of earning a satisfactory profit will diminish if you fail to achieve a reasonable sales volume. Remember there is the danger of losing customers to substitute products if you and your competitors do not create sufficient awareness of the industry's products through promotional efforts. This would mean neither you nor your *Merlin* competitors would reach the sales potential forecasted for the industry. You and your competitors can also lose sales to substitute products if the whole industry invests too little in product quality. Your task then is to design a marketing program that is both effective and efficient. For a marketing program to be successful, it must generate the demand you desire at the lowest possible cost.

As with almost any product, the promotion of your *Merlin* products can reach a point of diminishing returns. As you raise your levels of advertising, more potential customers become aware of your products. Unfortunately, awareness does not guarantee a purchase. At some point, additional expenditures on advertising will result in smaller increases in the number of sales of that product. Determining *when* you have reached this point is a problem all companies face and will be a continual challenge for your company.

Sales force. Each of your sales representatives is assigned exclusively to sell one product in one territory. This means that you must make decisions regarding your sales force for each of the six product-territory combinations independently. You begin the simulation with three sales representatives in each of the three territories for Product 1, and with five sales representatives in each of the three territories for Product 2. Each salesperson earns a base salary of $5,000 per quarter, plus a commission. The amount of the commission is also a decision you will make. The effort put forth by a salesperson is, of course, affected by the size of the commission. You will also make decisions on whether to hire or fire salespeople. It costs $8,000 to hire and train a new sales representative. Salespeople do not contribute to sales during the quarter in which they are hired and they cannot be transferred from one territory to another.

Web Spending. Each quarter you must determine how much money you will spend to maintain and promote your company's Web site. Effective use of the Web may improve the service you provide to your retailers as well as serving as a source of sales and service information for your products. To avoid conflict with your retailers, you have decided that you will not sell directly from the Web. However, you can use your Web site to direct interested customers to the nearest dealer carrying your merchandise. If you choose to spend money for the Web, you will enhance the capabilities of your Web site and you will purchase banner advertising on other Web sites to lead potential customers to your site. Web spending is not product or territory specific; all money spent enhances your Web site and applies to the promotion of both of your products in all three territories. You may spend from $0 to $99,999 on the Web in a quarter.

Newspaper Advertising. You can choose to advertise your products through newspaper advertising. You place newspaper ads on a territory-by-territory basis — not on a national basis. Your decision determines how many newspaper ads (each is one-eighth of a page) you will run during each quarter. For each product and each territory you can purchase from 0 to 99 ads. Marketing scholars generally believe that newspaper advertising is best used for producing immediate results (that is, results in the quarter in which the ad is run). Newspaper advertising doesn't carry over to subsequent quarters.

Consumer Magazines. Like newspaper advertising, you also purchase consumer magazine advertisements on a territory-by-territory (rather than a national) basis. You must decide how many quarter-page ads to purchase for each product in each territory. Magazine advertising tends to have a more lasting benefit than newspaper ads, affecting sales not only in the quarter in which it is run, but also in the following quarter. As with newspaper ads, the number of ads that you can purchase must range from 0 to 99.

Trade Magazines. Rather than advertising directly to the ultimate consumer, trade magazines are distributed to, and read by people in the trade (that is, by the retailers of your product). Retailers tend to be keenly interested in developments taking place within their industry and read the articles and ads in the trade magazine to stay informed. As with consumer magazines, advertising in trade magazines has some "carry-over" effect – an ad in a trade magazine affects sales in the period in which the ad is placed as well as having an effect on the subsequent period. You must decide how many half-page ads (0 to 99) you will place for each product in each territory. If you choose to purchase trade ads, some of your money will be spent on various forms of sales promotional activities to the trade.

Advertising Message. You must choose from among five different advertising messages. You can choose to vary the message from product to product or from territory to territory. However, for a given product, you must use the same message for all forms of advertising (newspapers, consumer magazines, and trade magazines) within a territory. The advertising messages are:
1. Price – emphasizes the low price of your product.
2. Features – stresses the superior features of your product.
3. Quality – extols the superior quality of your product.
4. Service – points out the service advantage that your company provides. This message is most effective when a large sales force supports it.
5. Benefits – describes the benefits the consumer (or retailer) can expect to derive from using your product. Rather focusing on price, features, quality, or service the "benefits" message explains (or demonstrates) the value of using the product.

Not all messages are equal in effectiveness. Price may be an excellent message choice if the product is essentially a commodity with no important differences among competitive offerings or if consumers are motivated primarily by price. On the other hand, if the consumers in your target market are not price sensitive, price may be a poor message choice. Give careful consideration to the nature of your product and the characteristics of the people in your target market before selecting a message.

Select the advertising message that you want by clicking on the pull-down menu and making your choice. The effectiveness of your advertising message is strongly influenced by how accurately it matches reality. For example, if you are advertising features but your product has fewer features than the products of most of your competitors, your message will be relatively ineffective. Your advertising will be most effective if you select a message that emphasizes an area in which you have a competitive advantage.

Place

The channels of distribution for your products are fixed. You sell your products to retailers. In addition, the owners of our company have decided that you may not sell outside of the three territories during the time you manage the company.

OTHER DECISIONS

Process Cost Reduction

You can spend money on process improvements in an attempt to reduce the production cost of your products. You can employ your technical specialists to search for ways to lower the per-unit cost of your products. Your specialists, working with the supplier, may find ways to reduce the manufacturing cost of the product and/or the physical distribution cost of the product. To achieve process cost reductions, you must enter the amount you want to spend in the Process Improvement slot of the decision screen. As with Product Features, investing in process improvements is an uncertain venture. You may spend money in one or more periods without achieving any savings. However, the more you spend, the more likely it is that you will see a process improvement; expenditures are cumulative. Spending just a few more dollars the next period may result in a cost reduction. Once you achieve a cost savings, it will remain in effect for the duration of the exercise – even if you do not spend a single additional dollar on cost reductions. Note that the money you spend for process improvements for one product does not help the other product; the cost reductions for each product are completely independent. If you achieve a process improvement, the amount of the cost reduction will appear on your Product Cost Report and will go into effect for the next quarter.

Product Ordered from Sub-contractor

As stated earlier, your company engages in no manufacturing. A national manufacturer produces everything you sell. The base cost of the units you order is shown on the Cost Parameters screen. Note that the base cost does not reflect process improvement savings, nor does it show added costs for features or quality. To see what your net per unit cost is including process savings plus quality and features expenditures, see the Product Cost Report screen.

There is a one-quarter delay from when you place an order with the manufacturer for sub-contracted units and when you receive the units and have them available for sale. The spending on quality this quarter will affect the quality of the sub-contracted units *received this* quarter, *not* those ordered for next quarter.

You must estimate how much of each product you will sell in each territory and order an appropriate amount from your supplier. If you fail to order enough in any territory, you will, of course, lose sales. On the other hand, if you order too much, you will have excess inventory at the end the quarter and will be forced to pay a carrying cost. To minimize lost sales, most companies choose to order a few more units than they think will actually be sold – this excess is referred to as "safety stock". The determination of the number of units to order from your supplier constitutes a critical set of decisions. Take great care to avoid calculation or data-entry errors.

Marketing Research and Demand Estimates

Marketing Research. Each quarter you may purchase marketing research information to see what your competitors are doing. Information is available on virtually all aspects of the marketing mix. It is wise to be informed about how your competitors' actions compare to yours. When you buy information about your competitors' actions, two options are available to you: 1) you may purchase information for all competitors in your industry; or 2) you can spend fewer dollars and purchase information for up to three competitors. If you decide to purchase marketing research information, first select whether you want All Companies or just Selected Companies. If you choose Selected Companies, enter the company numbers of the company or companies for which you want information. (The Cost Parameters Screen displays the cost of the marketing research information.) Then use your mouse and left-click on the research items you wish to order. In addition to the reports on the decisions your competitors are making, you can also purchase a report showing the actual number of units sold for each company (not including stockouts). This report is separate and different from the Industry Performance Report you will receive without cost each quarter. The Industry Performance Report only shows the sales *revenues* (i.e., price times the number of units sold) for each competitor operating in your industry.

You will receive any marketing research information you purchase only *after* you process the quarter in which they were purchased. You can see this when you view the Marketing Research Report for the quarter in which you purchased the information. For example, if you buy marketing research on price for Product 1 in Quarter 2, you will be able to view this information after Quarter 2 has been processed by selecting 2 from the Quarter menu and then selecting Marketing Research – P1 from the Reports menu.

Demand Estimates (Future Sales Potential). Each quarter you have the opportunity to purchase estimates for the demand for your products. Each demand estimate you buy provides information for one of your products in one territory. Future demand for a product is vitally important to a company because it can help determine how many units of each product you should order from your supplier. You may have difficulty predicting demand if you do not purchase a demand estimate because the sales of many products are seasonal (that is, some quarters typically will have greater sales than other quarters) and general market conditions change over time. You can purchase a research report that shows future sales potential for the products up to four quarters in advance of the quarter in which you are operating. You can choose which of the next four quarters you want to buy. Notice that there are two opportunities to purchase this information each quarter. This allows you to buy information for two different future quarters at the same time. Enter the number of the quarter for which you want information on the Marketing and Marketing Research Screen. If you enter the number of a quarter that is beyond four quarters in the future, an error message will appear on your screen.

The numbers you receive when you buy demand estimates represent the *total combined demand* (in units) for all companies in the industry for a given territory. If you multiply this total industry demand by your anticipated market share, you will have an estimate of the total sales potential for your product in that territory. For example, assume there are twelve companies in your industry and the demand estimate for Territory 1is 360,000 units. If your marketing effort (price, advertising expenditures, etc.) is average for your industry, you could anticipate capturing about 8.3333% (100% ÷ 12 companies) of all units sold in the industry. That is, you could expect to sell about 30,000 units (360,000 x .08333) of Product 1, in Territory 1 in that quarter. However, if one of your goals is to achieve a large market share and *if you market your product very aggressively* (low price, heavy advertising, etc.), you might anticipate, say, a 15% market share. In this case, you expect to sell about 54,000 units (360,000 x .15). You must keep in mind that this goal is greater than the average demand of 30,000, so to sell this amount requires a marketing effort greater than at least some of your competitors. Put simply, the higher the market share that you intend to achieve, the greater the effort you will have to put into marketing your product relative to your competitors. Remember, at some point the cost of this marketing effort will outweigh the benefits that come from the increased sales volume. In general, spend more money on the marketing factors that matter most and less money on those marketing factors that matter least.

> *Note:* See "Demand for Your Products" in Chapter 4 for demand estimates for *Quarter 1*. (The demand estimates for Quarter 1 represent average unit sales for *a single company* rather than total combined demand for all companies in the industry.)

You will have to decide what market research information is and is not valuable for managing your company. Careful use of this information can provide you with clues to the relative efficiency of your marketing efforts. You may also glean information about your competitors' strategies from these reports and use them to update your strategies or to make decisions that preempt their competitive actions.

SALES FORECAST ESTIMATE

The *Merlin* simulation allows you to make an estimate of demand for each of your products in the upcoming quarter of operation. In each input box of the Product Decision screens for Product 1 and

Product 2, enter a number between 0 and 99,999 that is your best estimate of the sales volume you think you will achieve for the product in the territory.

Exhibit 6.1

Decisions - Product 1		Territory 1	Territory 2	Territory 3
Price	($)	19.00	19.00	19.00
Newspaper Ads	(#)	15	15	15
Consumer Magazine Ads	(#)	10	10	10
Trade magazine Ads	(#)	12	12	12
Ad Message		Service	Service	Service
Sales Reps:				
Hire	(#)	0	0	0
Fire	(#)	0	0	0
Commission	(%)	3	3	3
Product Quality	($/Unit)	0.00	(For all territories)	
Web Spending	($)	8000	(For all territories and both products)	
Sales Forecast	(#)	31800	14600	39600
Product Ordered	(#)	55000	25000	65000
Product Features Development	($)	0		
Process Improvement	($)	0		
ST Loan Request	($)	700000		

Base your sales forecast estimate on the marketing mix you have chosen for this quarter. You need to adjust this estimate according to what you expect your competitors to do, the *Merlin* economic climate, and general demand for the product.

Once you enter your forecast estimates, the *Merlin* program uses these numbers to generate reports showing what would happen *if you actually sell the amounts you forecasted*. These reports allow you to see the effect of your decisions on your operating costs and net income, whether you need to request a short-term loan, and what your overall financial picture would be for the quarter. You can also see what your ending inventories would be. As a minimum, you should examine both worst-case and expected sales forecast estimates.

Forecast Reports vs. Actual Reports. Remember, the reports you see when you enter a forecast estimate are *projected* reports and are labeled as forecasts on the report screens and any printouts you generate. *These reports are only as good as your estimate of the demand for your products.* All of these projected reports are based on the sales forecast estimates you enter. There is no guarantee that you will actually sell what you estimate. You will not be warned if you enter wildly unrealistic forecast estimates; even impossible forecast estimates will generate reports showing the projected results. Actual sales are determined by the *Merlin* program *after* you have processed your decisions for that quarter and moved on to the next quarter. At that time, the reports are labeled as "actual" reports to distinguish them from the forecasted reports. If you have misjudged your competitors' actions or the general market demand for the two products, your forecasted sales can be considerably different from your actual sales. If this is the case, your forecasted results will not resemble your actual results. This means your ability to plan your actions and predict your results is highly dependent upon your ability to forecast accurately.

Remember two things about your sales forecast estimates. First, the sales forecast estimates you enter have no effect on your actual sales in a quarter. The *Merlin* program does not consider your sales forecast estimates when determining actual sales of a product. The program only considers the features, quality, price, promotion, and total market demand for a product when allocating sales. Second, *Merlin* will not warn you when your sales forecasts are unrealistic. It is your responsibility to understand your marketplace, using both quantitative methods and intuitive skills to make a reasoned prediction of what your products' sales volumes will be.

Note that not only are your demand estimates vitally important for your planning, but part of your performance in the simulation is tied directly to the accuracy of your sales forecast estimates. Therefore, it is in your best interests to work hard to develop an understanding of your industry and of how your decisions affect the demand for your products.

Short-Term Loan

Situations may arise when you expect your spending to exceed the amount of cash you have on hand. When you believe this will occur, you may request a short-term loan. Look at the Cash Flow Statement to determine what your cash needs are for the quarter. Then enter your decision for the amount you wish to borrow. If you take out a short-term loan, The Cost Parameters Screen displays the interest rate that you will be charged. The entire of amount of the loan will be repaid automatically at the end of the quarter following that in which it is borrowed. If you fail to anticipate your cash needs correctly and either don't borrow at all or don't borrow enough, you will be granted an emergency loan automatically, but you will be charged double the interest rate. So, plan carefully.

Note that you do not have unlimited resources. The maximum amount of anticipated debt that you can incur in any quarter is $2,999,999. If you attempt to borrow $3 million or more, you will get a message stating that you have exceeded the limit and the program will not permit you to proceed. Also be aware that as you enter your decisions the program keeps a running total of your cash position. If your decisions result in a situation where your cash payments exceed your anticipated cash receipts by $3 million or more, the program will not permit you to exit until you have corrected the problem. This is true *even if you do not take out a short-term loan*. If your expenditures are too high (that is, if they would result in an expected cash deficiency of $3 million or more), you must reduce your expenditures before the program will accept your decisions and allow you exit. It is worth repeating that if your expenditures exceed your anticipated receipts, you should request a short-term loan. If you fail to request a loan, the program will lend you the money needed to make up the difference, but you will pay double the normal interest rate.

It is important to recognize that you can incur a loan even if you enter "0" on your decision form. If your expenditures exceed your cash on hand, you will automatically be granted a loan (at a high interest rate) despite the fact that you did not intend to take out a loan.

CHAPTER 7

MERLIN REPORTS

After you process each set of decisions, you will receive a number of reports that will show the results of those decisions. You can view these reports and those of previous quarters that have been processed by using the Select Quarter option under File on the Main Menu or by using the Quarter menu and then choosing the number for the quarter you desire. Chapter 3 explains how to view and print reports. Remember, when you start the *Merlin* program, it automatically loads the *next* quarter's decision screens and associated reports. If you want to access the quarter that was just processed or an earlier quarter, use the Select Quarter option or the Quarter menu to move back to those reports.

In this chapter we will provide a description of each *Merlin* report that you can access on your company disk. We will work with Quarter 2 reports so that you have an idea of what your company might look like during the play of the simulation. When you process your Quarter 2 decisions, the program will automatically move to Quarter 3. You must select Quarter 2 to see your reports. The reports provided by *Merlin* include:

- Historical information reports
  - Decisions Report (one for Product 1 and one for Product 2)
  - Marketing Research Decisions Report (one for Product 1 and one for Product 2)
  - Product 1 Report (Product 1)
  - Product 2 Report (Product 2)
- Marketing reports
  - Sales & Administration Summary Report
  - Marketing Research – Product 1
  - Marketing Research – Product 2
- Operations reports
  - Product Cost Report
  - Inventory Report (for Territories 1, 2, and 3)
- Financial reports
  - Income Statement
  - Balance Sheet
  - Cash Flow Statement
- Industry performance reports
  - Quarter Performance Report
  - Game To Date Performance Report
- Information Menu Reports
  - Cost Parameters
  - Bulletin

> **Note: In performance reports for *Merlin Solo*, you are always Company 1**

HISTORICAL INFORMATION REPORTS

Decisions Reports and Marketing Research Decisions Reports

Four of the *Merlin* reports show the decisions you made in Quarter 2. These are the two decisions reports (one for Product 1 and one for Product 2) and the two marketing research reports (one for Product 1 and one for Product 2). Exhibits 7.1 and 7.2 are examples of these reports for the decisions made for Product 1.

Exhibit 7.1

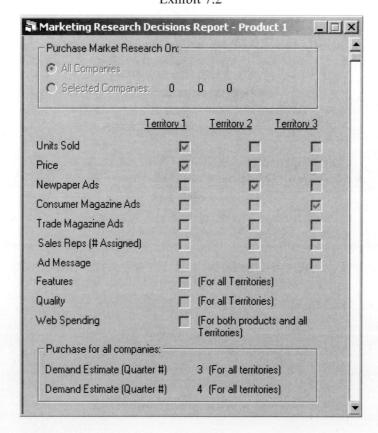

Exhibit 7.2

Product Reports

The two Product Reports (one for Product 1 and one for Product 2) provide information for: (1) the expenditures incurred given the decisions you made in Quarter 2; and (2) the number of sales representatives you had available as of the end of Quarter 2. Exhibit 7.3 is an example of this report for Product 1. As you can see on this product report, the total selling expenses for Product 1 were $352,744 and there were three sales representatives in each territory. Note that one additional sales rep was hired in Quarter 2 for Territory 1 – the hiring and training expense appear as $8,000 on the Product 1 Report but that representative does not become effective until Quarter 3. (If you looked at the Product 1 Report for Quarter 3, you would see four sales representatives for Territory 1.)

Exhibit 7.3

SELLING		Territory 1	Territory 2	Territory 3	Total
Product Features	($)	1333	1333	1333	4000
Process Improvement	($)	400	400	400	1200
Web Spending	($)	543	195	762	1500
Newspaper Ads	($)	37500	27500	37500	102500
Consumer Magazine Ads	($)	40000	32000	40000	112000
Trade Magazine Ads	($)	24000	12000	24000	60000
Sales Reps:					
Assigned	($)	15000	15000	15000	45000
Hired	($)	8000	0	0	8000
Commissions paid	($)	6442	3084	9018	18544
SubTotal	($)	133218	91512	128014	352744
Sales Reps Available	(#)	3	3	3	

MARKETING REPORTS

Sales & Administration Summary

This report shows your marketing and administration expenses (See Exhibit 7.4). Each entry for Product 1 and Product 2 represents the combined costs for all three territories for that product. The very last line of the report shows the number of features that each of your products had as of the end of Quarter 2. The company represented in this report has not invested enough money yet to achieve a feature for either of its products.

As you can see in Exhibit 7.4, this company had sales costs of $352,744 and marketing research costs of $12,000 for Product 1. In addition, Product 1 was charged $20,347 for Office Expense. This Office Expense charge is a company-wide charge and is not related specifically to either Product 1 or Product 2. You incur this expense simply to keep your company operating. Unlike your sales or marketing research costs, this is an overhead charge that occurs every quarter regardless of how much or how little you produce or sell. On the Sales & Administration Summary (and, therefore, also on the Income Statement), Office Expense is allocated proportionally to the two products based on the cost of goods sold for each product. For example, in this case, the total cost of goods sold for both products combined was $1,201,018 (shown on the Income Statement). Office expense was allocated between the two products based on the fact that the cost of goods sold for Product 1 was 67.83% of the total cost of goods sold ($814,594 ÷ $1,201,018), and Product 2 cost of goods sold was 32.17% of total cost of goods sold (i.e.,

$386,424 ÷ $1,201,018). Consequently, $20,347 of the total Office Expense of $29,999 was charged to Product 1 (67.83% * $29,999 = $20,347). Similarly, $9,652 of the total Office Expense was charged to Product 2 (32.17% * $29,999 = $9,652).

Exhibit 7.4

Sales & Administration Summary				
SELLING		Product 1	Product 2	Total
Product Features Spending	($)	4000	0	4000
Process Improvement Spending	($)	1200	3000	4200
Web Spending	($)	1500	1500	3000
Newspaper Ads	($)	102500	125000	227500
Consumer Magazine Ads	($)	112000	144000	256000
Trade Magazine Ads	($)	60000	70000	130000
Sales Reps	($)	53000	91000	144000
Commissions Paid	($)	18544	30055	48599
Subtotal	($)	352744	464555	817299
ADMINISTRATIVE				
Office Expense	($)	20347	9652	29999
Marketing Research	($)	12000	8000	20000
Fines	($)	0	0	0
Refunds	($)	0	0	0
TOTAL S & A EXPENSES		385091	482207	867298
Product Features	(Total #)	0	0	

Marketing Research Reports – Product 1 and Product 2

The Market Research Report shows information you purchased regarding your competitors' actions as well as estimates of potential sales (i.e., market demand) in future quarters. You can access a particular marketing research report as long as you select the quarter in which you purchased the information. *You cannot view these reports in a quarter that has not yet been processed* (i.e., a quarter in which you are forecasting results versus viewing actual reports). For example, if you purchased the information in Quarter 3, you must select Quarter 2 from the Quarter menu to be able to view the report.

In the marketing research report shown in Exhibit 7.5, information was purchased for all competitors and for all variables in Territory One – the actual Quarter 3 units sold by all competitors in Territory 1; the prices charged by all competitors in Territory 1; the quality expenditures; etc. In addition, demand estimates were purchased for the next two periods, Quarters 4 and 5. These demand estimates represent the *total anticipated unit sales for the entire industry* for Product 1 in Territory 1 for each of these two quarters. The unit sales achieved *by your company* will be affected by your marketing efforts and by the number of companies in your industry.

Exhibit 7.5

Co. #	Units Sold	Price	Features	Quality	Web	News	Cons. Mags	Trade Mags	Sales Reps	Ad Msg
					Territory 1					
1	4648	37.00	0	0.00	8000	15	10	12	3	Service
2	33013	20.11	3	0.60	14347	11	11	10	5	Quality
3	39177	18.41	0	0.14	28789	17	8	9	3	Price
4	31399	19.35	1	0.56	6000	9	3	6	5	Service
5	38700	18.71	0	0.27	17123	18	12	13	4	Features
6	30237	19.49	1	0.57	13385	8	6	8	5	Quality
7	37317	18.73	0	0.16	25000	12	9	9	3	Price
8	31695	19.38	1	0.56	6000	10	3	6	5	Service
9	43342	18.57	1	0.28	24751	19	12	15	4	Features
10	31840	19.65	2	0.55	14636	14	10	7	4	Quality
11	46339	18.44	0	0.17	29012	18	12	13	3	Price
12	29487	19.35	1	0.64	6000	6	3	7	6	Service

Demand Estimate for Quarter   4   414000   Demand Estimate for Quarter   5   386400

Territory 1   Territory 2   Territory 3

OPERATIONS REPORTS

Two of the *Merlin* reports show the status of your operations. These are the Product Cost Report and the Inventory Report. Both of these reports are important to the successful management of your marketing operations. If the cost of your products is too high, you can forfeit profits even though you achieve your desired sales goals. Similarly, if you do not properly control your inventory levels, you can end up with poor results. For example, you could generate a demand for your product, but not have those items available for the customer to purchase. Alternatively, you could carry inventory levels far greater than are necessary and have to pay the expense of maintaining those excess inventories. We discuss each of these two reports in more detail, next.

Product Cost Report

The top line of the Product Cost Report (see Exhibit 7.6) shows the base cost per unit for each of the products ordered from your supplier. This price is adjusted for any process savings or quality or features costs that you have achieved. The last line of the report shows the actual per unit cost that you paid for each of your products in Quarter 2. The company shown in Exhibit 7.5 has not yet achieved any process savings or features, nor is it spending any money for quality on Product 1, so its base cost and total cost are the same for Product 1. You will note that the company is spending $0.38 per unit for Product 2. You can see what your product costs for Quarter 3 will be by selecting Quarter 3 and looking at the Product Cost Report

Exhibit 7.6

Product Cost Report		Product 1	Product 2
Base Product Cost	($/Unit)	11.00	27.00
Less Process Savings	($/Unit)	0.00	0.00
Plus Features Costs	($/Unit)	0.00	0.00
Plus Quality Costs	($/Unit)	0.00	0.38
Total Product Cost	($/Unit)	11.00	27.38

Inventory Report

The Inventory Report (Exhibit 7.7) displays your inventory position for both products and for all three territories, both in units and in dollars. The company shown in Exhibit 7.7 began Quarter 2 with 25,783 units of Product 1 in Territory 1. In Quarter 1, the company ordered 55,000 units, so these units were received in Quarter 2. Thus, the company had 83,783 units available for sale during the second quarter. The company sold 26,840 units in Territory 1, Quarter 2, and was left with an ending inventory of 53,943 units at the end of the Quarter 2. These 53,943 units, of course, become the beginning inventory for Quarter 3.

The Inventory Report is an important tool because it provides the information you need to maintain reasonable inventory levels. If you carry too much inventory, your carrying costs will cut into your profits – in this case, the carrying costs for bringing 25,783 units of Product 1 (in Territory 1) into Quarter 2, totaled $30,940 and this cost was subtracted directly from gross profits on the Income Statement. Quarter 2's, ending inventory of 53,943 will produce a carrying cost of $64,732 (53,943 x $1.20) on the Quarter 3 Inventory Report. *[Note that the carrying costs appearing on the Inventory Report are for the units carried forward from the previous period – i.e., on units in Beginning Inventory.]* On the other hand, if you fail to carry sufficient inventory, you will stock out and this will appear on your Inventory Report as lost sales. The lost sales line reflects the additional sales revenue you could have received during the quarter if you had sufficient goods available for sale. Your inventory together with your sales forecast estimates form the basis for determining how many units you must order from your supplier for the next quarter. Your challenge, then, is to keep inventories low to avoid excessive storage charges, while avoiding the opportunity costs of stocking out and having lost sales.

Note that when you look at your Inventory Report for a quarter in which you are making decisions (rather than a period that has already been processed), the *sales forecast estimate* that you enter on your Decisions – Product 1 form will determine the "units sold" and will affect the "ending inventory" line of your Inventory Report. *Of course, if your estimates are incorrect, your actual inventory levels may differ markedly from those shown on this forecasted report.*

Exhibit 7.7

Inventory Report						

Territory 1

	Product 1			Product 2		
	Units	$/Unit	Value	Units	$/Unit	Value
Beginning Inventory	25783	11.00	283613	4437	27.00	119799
Unit Received	55000	11.00	605000	11000	27.00	297000
Units Available for Sale	80783	11.00	888613	15437	27.00	416799
Units Sold	26840	11.00	295240	6339	27.00	171153
Ending Inventory	53943	11.00	593373	9098	27.00	245646
Lost Sales	0	11.00	0	0	27.00	0
Inventory Cost	25783	1.20	30940	4437	2.20	9761

Territory 1	Territory 2	Territory 3

INCOME STATEMENT

The purpose of the Income Statement for any quarter is to show the amount of profit or loss that occurred as a result of your company's operations that quarter. Exhibit 7.8 shows the Income Statement for the sample company's Quarter 2 operations. On the Income Statement, the first three lines show the sales revenue by territory for Products 1 and 2 for the quarter. The next line gives the total sales revenues for each of the products. In Quarter 2, total sales revenues were $1,407,026 for Product 1 and $1987,528 for Product 2. The combined total for the two products was $2,394,554.

The various costs of running the business that quarter are then subtracted from the total sales revenues. The Cost of Goods Sold is the first item subtracted. The dollar amount of the Cost of Goods Sold comes directly from the Units Sold line of the Inventory Report. It is the sum of the dollar amounts (Value) of the three territories. This figure, ($814,594 for Product 1 and $386,424 for Product 2) reflects the cost of goods that were sold for Quarter 2.

The Gross Profit line shows whether your operations generated a profit during the quarter. This is the money left after subtracting costs paid to your subcontractor (Cost of Goods Sold) from your sales revenues. Gross profit does not reflect all the costs of running your company. It shows the money you have available to pay for the marketing, administrative, and warehouse costs associated with running your company and promoting your products. Combined Gross Profit for Products 1 and 2 was $1,193,536 in Quarter 2.

The charges for selling and administrative expenses come from the Sales & Administration Summary Report. The Inventory Carrying Costs are brought in directly from the Inventory Cost line of the Inventory Report and are the sum of all three territories for each product. In Quarter 2 the total S&A costs were $867,298 while the Inventory Carrying Costs were $99,032.

Exhibit 7.8

	Product 1	Product 2	Total
Sales:			
Territory 1	509960	437391	947351
Territory 2	183103	233427	416530
Territory 3	713963	316710	1030673
Total Sales	1407026	987528	2394554
Cost of Goods Sold	814594	386424	1201018
Gross Profit	592432	601104	1193536
S & A	385091	482207	867298
Inventory Carrying Costs	74423	24609	99032
Operating Profit	132918	94288	227206
Net Interest	37216	17655	54871
Profit Before Taxes	95702	76633	172335
Income Taxes Payable			86167
Net Income			86167

After deducting costs for Sales & Administration expenses and Inventory Carrying Costs, the Income Statement shows an Operating Profit of $227,206 resulting from running your business. Your Operating Profit (Loss) does not include the cost of loans. The Net Interest line shows the cost of borrowing money to run the company. Like Office Expense (described in the Sales & Administration Summary Report), interest expenses are allocated between the two products according to the cost of goods sold for each product. Your interest expenses include both interest on the short-term loan you requested (on the Decisions – Product 1 form) plus the interest fee for any emergency loan advanced by the program to enable you to cover your cash requirements for the quarter. (For greater detail on emergency loans, see the explanation of the Cash Flow Statement.) The interest rate that you are charged for the short-term loan can be found on the Cost Parameters screen under the Info menu option. The Cost Parameters screen shows the *annual* rate, so your rate for each quarter is one-fourth of this annual rate.

The Cash Flow Statement (discussed later) shows the breakdown of your interest charges. By keeping the costs of financing your business out of the Operating Profit calculation, you can more readily see whether problems that develop originate in how you operate your business versus the financing of these operations. It is not uncommon for a business to be profitable in making and selling its product, but to end up losing money because it borrowed large sums to develop the business. Knowing the cause of your problem is the first step in being able to solve it.

In Quarter 2 total interest expenses amounted to $54,871. This expense is subtracted from Operating Profit to yield Profit Before Taxes. Note that interest charges for money borrowed are reflected in your Income Statement the quarter after they were incurred.

The Income Taxes Payable line shows the taxes you must pay on any profits you earned that quarter. The current tax rate you must pay is 50%. If you lose money in a quarter, you will not have to pay any taxes for that quarter. In addition, if you earn a profit in other quarters during that same year, your tax payments will be reduced in recognition of the loss. The calculation of whether you are due any tax refunds because of losses you incurred earlier is done in the last quarter of each year. Any year-end tax reconciliations will occur in Quarters 4, 8, 12, 16, etc.

BALANCE SHEET

The next report is the Balance Sheet (Exhibit 7.9). It shows the financial status of your company at the end of the quarter. The Balance Sheet is a snapshot summary indicating the Assets and Liabilities of the company at the end of that accounting period.

Exhibit 7.9

Balance Sheet			
ASSETS		**LIABILITIES AND OWNERS EQUITY**	
Cash	0	Short-Term Loans Payable	2092525
Accounts Receivable	1436732	Taxes Payable	86167
Finished Goods	2080213		
		Owners Equity	1338253
TOTAL ASSETS	3516946	TOTAL LIABILITIES & OWNERS EQUITY	3516945

The Balance Sheet also shows the net value (i.e., net worth) of your company. This is the liquidated value of the business if it "closed up shop" and sold everything to pay for everything it owed. Whether the owners would actually collect this amount of money would depend on whether they could sell their assets for book value (i.e., the value of the assets shown on the Balance Sheet). The owners might end up selling the company's assets for more or less than their stated book value. This is similar to selling a used car. How much the potential buyer wants the car and what shape it is in will affect whether the car is sold at, above, or below a car dealer's "Blue Book" price. The same kind of situation holds for the seller of assets of a business. The only asset that is worth exactly what is shown on the Balance Sheet is Cash. And even this account is open to bargaining if the company does business outside the United States and has to deal with changing rates of exchange for the dollar. This problem does not exist in *Merlin*. All your revenues are from domestic sales.

Assets

The Current Assets shown on the left side of the Balance Sheet represent those assets that can be converted into cash within the next business period. (In *Merlin*, the next business period is the next quarter of operation.) They include Cash, Accounts Receivable, and Finished Goods inventory. Accounts Receivable on the Balance Sheet show all the money owed by customers who have bought your product but who have not yet paid. The Cash and Accounts Receivable shown here are different from those shown on the Cash Flow Statement (discussed in the next section).

Because you sub-contract all of your production, you have no long-term assets to reflect on your Balance Sheet. In Quarter 2, the Total Assets of your company were valued at $3,516,946.

Liabilities and Owners' Equity

The Liabilities shown on the Balance Sheet reflect the money the company owes others with which it does business. Your liabilities include short-term loan payments you have to make to your bank, and taxes you have to pay to the government. As of the end of Quarter 2, the sample company owed $2,092,525 in short-term loans and $86,167 for taxes, for total liabilities of $2,178,692.

Subtracting Total Liabilities from Total Assets shows the amount of equity the owners and any other investors have accumulated in the business. The equity accounts reflect what the company would be worth if the company stopped operating the business, sold off all its assets at book value and paid off all its liabilities, leaving the remainder (i.e., the Owners' Equity) for the owners of the company. At the end of Quarter 2, the sample company had an Owners' Equity value of $1,338,253. This is the difference between Total Assets ($3,516,946) and Total Liabilities ($2,178,692).

CASH FLOW STATEMENT

The Cash Flow Statement provides information on the cash your company received and paid out this quarter. Exhibit 7.10 shows the impact of decisions made in Quarter 2 on your company's cash flow for that quarter. Your cash receipts include Cash on Hand remaining from the last quarter's operations and the Collection of Accounts Receivable.

Exhibit 7.10

The Cash Flow Statement differs from the Income Statement, which shows the dollar value of products you sold and the profits you earned during the quarter. The Cash Flow Statement shows the *actual* cash you received this quarter. This includes money you collected from Accounts Receivable. The Accounts Receivable on the Cash Flow Statement shows the amount of cash received from accounts owed to the company for sales made in the prior quarter.

Cash Flow Statement

CASH RECEIPTS:	
Cash On Hand	0
Collection of A/R	2517105
TOTAL CASH RECEIPTS	2517105
CASH PAYMENTS:	
Product Cost Expense	2297000
S & A Expense	867298
Inventory Carrying Cost	99032
Short-Term Interest	54871
Short-Term Loan Payment	1097422
Income Taxes Paid	194006
TOTAL CASH PAYMENTS	4609629
NET CASH FLOW	-2092525
ST LOAN GRANTED	2092525
NET CASH BALANCE	0

Cash Receipts

Merlin companies sell their products on credit. Normal terms are net 90 days, but some customers will pay cash for the products. For any given quarter 40% of the sales revenues will be collected immediately, with the remaining 60% collected in the next quarter. This means the receivables from last quarter (i.e., 60% of last quarter's sales) are added to 40% of this quarter's sales to produce the cash inflow from sales for this quarter. In Quarter 2, your company collected $2,517,105 of your outstanding Accounts Receivable – 40% of Quarter 2 sales of $2,394,554 plus 60% of Quarter 1 sales of $2,598,805. Because of this delayed collection of sales revenues, managing your cash flow requires planning.

Having this delay between when the company sells its products and when it receives the cash for these sales is typical for almost every business. Just think of how often you pay for your purchases with a credit card. You leave the store with the merchandise and the store has only a slip of paper saying the credit card company will send the cash later. Yet the storeowner has had to pay out *cash* for employee wages and advertising before you even entered the store. Consequently, learning how to manage your cash flow can be a key to achieving success for any organization.

Cash Payments

Cash Payments reflect the payments your company made during the quarter. The first line under Cash Payments shows your product cost expense. This is the payment you make for the goods you received from your supplier that quarter. It is the sum for both products and all three territories. You pay on a cash-on-delivery basis. This means you pay your supplier for goods in the quarter you receive them, not when you order them. In Quarter 2 you paid your supplier $2,297,000.

Selling and administrative payments come from the Sales & Administration Summary report. In Quarter 2, this totaled $867,298. Inventory carrying cost amounted to $99,032.

Short-Term Interest shows the interest payment made for money borrowed last quarter. The sample company's interest payments were $54,871. The Short-Term Loan Payment line shows the amount repaid on any short-term loan you have outstanding. You always pay the entire amount of the short-term loan the quarter after you receive it. The sample company was granted a short-term loan of $1,097,422 in Quarter 1 and repaid that loan in Quarter 2.

The Income Taxes Paid line shows the taxes you had to pay. This is different from Income Taxes Payable on the Income Statement because those are not paid out in cash until the next quarter of operation. So this line represents your tax obligation for profits earned in the preceding quarter. For Quarter 2 the sample company's tax payment was $194,006, the amount shown as the Income Taxes Payable on the Quarter 1 Income Statement.

Net Cash Flow and Short-Term Loan

The last three lines on the Cash Flow Statement are Net Cash Flow, Short-Term Loan Granted, and Net Cash Balance. Net Cash Flow is the result of subtracting Total Cash Payments from Cash Receipts. Net Cash Flow reflects the cash generated by this quarter's operations or, if a minus figure, the cash needed to finance the operations. If you need a short-term loan to cover a cash shortfall, you must be sure to determine and request the amount of cash you need accurately. *Merlin* places a premium on cash planning. Any time your company does not have a zero or positive cash balance, the program will provide you with an automatic emergency loan to bring your cash balance up to zero. The interest rate for an emergency loan will be double the normal rate for short-term loans. It is important to recognize that *this higher interest rate applies to the total loan granted*, not just to the difference between the amount you requested and the amount actually needed. Emergency loans are charged a higher than normal interest rate to cover the cost of making the loan on such short notice. It is important that you consider your cash needs carefully and plan appropriately.

Your company has a "regular" credit limit of $3 million. If you request a short-term loan in excess of $3 million or if your decisions result in a cash position that would require a loan of more than $3 million, your interest rate will double.

When you look at the Cash Flow Statement in a period for which you are making decisions (rather than a historical period), the Net Cash Flow and Short-Term Loan Granted lines will keep a running total of your cash needs. This cash position is based on your expenditures and the *sales forecast estimates* that you make. If your forecasts are inaccurate, your actual cash receipts will differ from those shown on your Cash Flow Statement. If you borrow just enough to yield a Net Cash Balance of zero, you may well have requested a short-term loan that is too small to cover all your cash needs for the upcoming quarter. You need to request a short-term loan that balances the risk of falling short of your actual cash needs (and incurring an emergency loan), against the expense of paying interest charges on money you do not really need.

INDUSTRY PERFORMANCE REPORTS

Note: In performance reports for *Merlin Solo*, you are always Company 1

Quarter Performance Report

In addition to reports on the performance of your individual company, you will also receive two industry performance reports. Both reports will provide you with information for all companies in your *Merlin* industry on four factors: sales revenues, net income, return on sales (ROS), and the accuracy of each company's sales forecasts. One of the industry performance reports shows the performance of all the companies on these four factors *for the current quarter*. The other report shows a *game-to-date summary* on these factors.

Exhibit 7.11 shows an example of just the Quarter Performance Report. We will use this example to discuss each of the four performance factors and explain how the *Merlin* program calculates the points assigned to each company in the PTS AWRD columns.

The Four Performance Factors.

For each of the four factors, the report shows each company's performance, plus a ranking and an evaluation of that performance. The column under each heading — Sales, Income, etc. — shows what each company achieved for that factor in that quarter. Figures shown for the sales revenues, net income, and return on sales factors indicate each company's actual performance on these factors. For example, Company 1 had sales revenues for Quarter 2 of $2,394,554 and net income of $86,167. Both of these figures are taken from the company's Income Statement for the quarter. Company 1's ROS (i.e., return on sales) was 3.6%, which indicates the company's net income was 3.6% of its sales of $2,394,554.

Exhibit 7.11

COMP	SALES	PTS AWRD	INCOME	PTS AWRD	ROS	PTS AWRD	FORECAST ERRORS	PTS AWRD	OVERALL PTS	RANK
1	2394554	13	86167	12	3.6	10	14634	10*	45	12
2	2859595	16	176324	24	6.2	18	25513	6	63	8
3	3888487	22	323727	44	8.3	24	23278	6	95	3
4	2744481	15	160934	22	5.9	17	30688	5	59	9
5	3642671	20	280916	38	7.7	22	14316	10*	90	4
6	2993977	17	205497	28	6.9	20	22811	6	70	6
7	3807911	21	319636	43	8.4	24*	15417	9	98	1
8	2667394	15	146319	20	5.5	16	38691	4	54	11
9	3709247	21	265698	36	7.2	20	16823	9	86	5
10	3107781	17	194521	26	6.3	18	17775	8	70	7
11	3915391	22*	326604	44*	8.3	24	24632	6	96	2
12	2663010	15	149973	20	5.6	16	35936	4	55	10
Ave	3199541		219693		6.7		23376			

For the sales forecast factor, the figure shows the *absolute* difference in unit sales between the *actual demand* generated by a company's marketing efforts and the sales *forecast* made by that company. The report does not make any distinction on whether the sales forecast was high or low. It is only concerned with how much the forecast differed from the actual demand generated for the company's products. Notice that it is actual *demand*, not actual sales, that is used to determine this factor. This means any sales lost due to stockouts will be included in determining the accuracy of a company's sales forecasting. For this factor the smallest error indicates the best performance. In Exhibit 7.11, Company 1 had combined total unit sales forecast errors for both products of 14,634 for Quarter 2.

Calculation of Points Awarded.

The Points Awarded (Pts Awrd) columns show the number of points awarded based on each company's performance on the four factors. The points awarded to each company for their performance on a particular factor are calculated based on (a) the maximum possible points that could be achieved for that factor and (b) the company's performance relative to the company with the best performance on that factor. In the example shown in Exhibit 7.11, the maximum number of points for each factor is as follows: Sales – 22 points; Net Income – 44 points; Return on Sales – 24 points; and Forecast Errors – 10 points. Thus, Net Income (having the greatest number of points) will carry the most weight in determining the overall rank of each company's performance for the period. The company with the best performance for the quarter on a particular factor receives the maximum number of points for that factor. (Note that the best performance on a factor is indicated by a * next to the number.) In this example, Company 11 had the highest income of any company for Quarter 2 ($326,604), so it was awarded the maximum of 44 points for this factor. Company 1 was awarded 12 points of the 44 point maximum for Income. This was calculated by dividing Company 1's income for the quarter by Company 11's quarterly income and then multiplying that by 44 ([86,167÷326,604] * 44). In this example, Company 1's income was 26.4% (86,167÷326,604) of the company which achieved the best income for the quarter (Company 11). Consequently, Company 1 received 26.4% of the maximum possible points (44) that could be achieved for that factor. This resulted in a Pts Awrd of 12 (26.4% * 44). In our example, Company 1 was awarded a total of 45 points for its performance in Quarter 2. It received 13 points for sales revenues, 12 points for income, 10 points for its ROS, and 10 points for its forecasting errors. This performance earned Company 1 a ranking of number 12 (last place) in the industry for that quarter.

The points awarded to an individual company on two of the factors, Sales and Forecast Errors, can range from 0 to the maximum allowable for that factor. In the case shown in Exhibit 7.11, the points awarded to Company 1 could have been anywhere from 0 to 22 for Sales and from 0 to 10 for Forecast Errors. However, the points awarded to an individual company on the other two factors, Income and ROS, can actually be negative. In Exhibit 7.11, every company performed well enough to achieve a positive score on all four factors. However, if a company had suffered a loss, the points awarded for Income and ROS would have been negative. In this example, the possible range of points for Income is –44 to +44 and, for ROS,   -26 to +26.

The maximum possible points for each of the four factors is determined by either the administrator or by the *Merlin* program. The only constraint on the allocation of the points is that the total of all starred points (the maximum points for an individual factor) for the four factors must equal exactly 100. This means if one factor is allocated 100 points, all other factors would have to be allocated 0 points. Usually at least a few points are allocated to each factor.

Game-to-Date Performance Report

As with the Quarter Performance Report, the Game-to-Date summary shows the total points awarded to a company based on the number of points it received on each of the four performance factors. (See Exhibit 7.12.) For the Game-to-Date report, these calculations are based on all quarters of operation. For the sales, net income, and sales forecast factors, the Game-to-Date report is an *accumulation* of the combined total of all quarters of operation. For the ROS factor, this report shows the *average* for all quarters of operation, rather than the total of the quarters. This allows a better comparison of game-to-date performance with current-quarter performance. The Game-to-Date summary also shows the rank of each company based on the total points it had been awarded.

Exhibit 7.12

Game To Date Peformance Report   _ □ ✕

COMP	SALES	PTS AWRD	INCOME	PTS AWRD	ROS	PTS AWRD	FORECAST ERRORS	PTS AWRD	OVERALL PTS	RANK
1	7800359	17	458753	25	5.9	18	19839	10*	70	7
2	8230814	17	508739	28	6.2	19	38774	5	70	8
3	10356140	22	791385	44	7.6	24	67293	3	92	2
4	7478189	16	389345	22	5.2	16	69688	3	56	10
5	9766532	21	690696	38	7.1	22	31119	6	87	4
6	8265976	18	523936	29	6.3	20	43088	5	71	6
7	10194020	22	794892	44*	7.8	24*	53047	4	93	1
8	7426169	16	368478	20	5.0	15	78328	3	54	12
9	9991088	21	675487	37	6.8	21	47915	4	84	5
10	8357568	18	483741	27	5.8	18	39414	5	67	9
11	10366320	22*	786888	44	7.6	23	68130	3	92	3
12	7491269	16	381527	21	5.1	16	69987	3	56	11
Ave	8810371		571156		6.4		52219			

INFO MENU REPORTS

Cost Parameters Report

Exhibit 7.13 lists the costs associated with your decisions. You should check your company's cost parameters regularly for any changes. Any of the costs can change during the course of the *Merlin* exercise. Get in the habit of checking your current costs every quarter. It is up to you to be knowledgeable regarding your company's costs. Not recognizing which costs have changed will be detrimental to your ability to manage your company efficiently.

Exhibit 7.13

Cost Parameters				
GENERAL COSTS		**MARKET RESEARCH COSTS**		
			Per Company	All Companies
News Ads ($ per 1/8 page)	2500	Units sold	200	2000
Consumer Mag Ads (per 1/4 page)	4000	Price	250	2000
Trade Mag Ads (per 1/2 page)	2000	Features	750	6000
Sales Reps Salary ($/quarter)	5000	Quality	750	6000
Sales Reps Hire/Train ($/quarter)	8000	Web Spending	750	6000
Product Base Cost P1	11.00	News Ads	250	2000
Product Base Cost P2	27.00	Consumer Mag Ads	250	2000
Inventory Carrying Cost P1	1.20	Trade Magazine Ads	250	2000
Inventory Carrying Cost P2	2.20	Sales Reps	250	2000
Administrative Expense	30000	Ad Message	400	4000
Features P1 Mfg ($ / unit)	0.10	Demand Estimates		2000
Features P2 Mfg ($ / unit)	0.30			
Short-Term Loan Rate (%)	10.0			

Bulletin

The Bulletin is the final screen in *Merlin*. The Bulletin is a message board. If your administrator has any information that he or she wishes to pass on to you, this is where that information will appear. The message can change any quarter, so it is a good idea to get in the habit of checking the Bulletin at the start of each new quarter.

You should now have a basic understanding of each of the *Merlin* reports that you will work with throughout the simulation exercise. The more you work with them, the greater your confidence should become in using them to manage your company. While these reports are simplistic compared to those of large, complex organizations, the principles for using the reports to gain insight into how to manage any company are similar. Learning how to analyze where your costs are coming from, and how to control these costs, is a key to working within any company. We hope and believe the challenges you face in this simulation experience will aid you in that process.

Good luck.

APPENDIX A

QUARTER 0 DECISIONS

Decisions Report - Product 1

		Territory 1	Territory 2	Territory 3
Price	($)	19.00	19.00	19.00
Newspaper Ads	(#)	15	15	15
Consumer Magazine Ads	(#)	10	10	10
Trade magazine Ads	(#)	12	12	12
Ad Message		Service	Service	Service
Sales Reps:				
Hire	(#)	0	0	0
Fire	(#)	0	0	0
Commission	(%)	3	3	3
Product Quality	($/Unit)	0.00 (For all territories)		
Web Spending	(#)	8000 (For all territories and both products)		
Sales Forecast	(#)	31800	14600	39600
Product Ordered	(#)	55000	25000	65000
Product Features Develoment	($)	0		
Process Improvement	($)	0		
ST Loan Request	($)	700000		

Decisions Report - Product 2

		Territory 1	Territory 2	Territory 3
Price	($)	69.00	69.00	69.00
Newspaper Ads	(#)	18	18	18
Consumer Magazine Ads	(#)	12	12	12
Trade magazine Ads	(#)	14	14	14
Ad Message		Service	Service	Service
Sales Reps:				
Hire	(#)	0	0	0
Fire	(#)	0	0	0
Commission	(%)	5	5	5
Product Quality	($/Unit)	0.00 (For all territories)		
Web Spending	(#)	8000 (For all territories and both products)		
Sales Forecast	(#)	7500	3700	5800
Product Ordered	(#)	11000	6000	9000
Product Features Develoment	($)	0		
Process Improvement	($)	0		

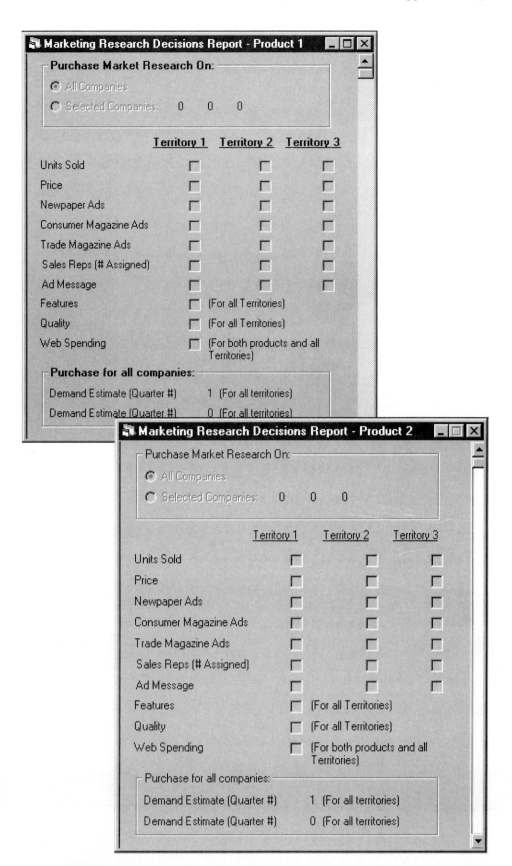

APPENDIX B
QUARTER 0 REPORTS

Product Cost Report

		Product 1	Product 2
Base Product Cost	($/Unit)	11.00	27.00
Less Process Savings	($/Unit)	0.00	0.00
Plus Features Costs	($/Unit)	0.00	0.00
Plus Quality Costs	($/Unit)	0.00	0.00
Total Product Cost	($/Unit)	11.00	27.00

Inventory Report

Territory 1

	Product 1			Product 2		
	Units	$/Unit	Value	Units	$/Unit	Value
Beginning Inventory	0	0.00	0	0	0.00	0
Unit Received	31800	11.00	349800	7500	27.00	202500
Units Available for Sale	31800	11.00	349800	7500	27.00	202500
Units Sold	31800	11.00	349800	7500	27.00	202500
Ending Inventory	0	11.00	0	0	27.00	0
Lost Sales	0	11.00	0	0	27.00	0
Inventory Cost	0	1.20	0	0	2.20	0

Territory 1	Territory 2	Territory 3

Product 1 Report

SELLING		Territory 1	Territory 2	Territory 3	Total
Newspaper Ads	($)	52500	52500	52500	157500
Consumer Magazine Ads	($)	50000	50000	50000	150000
Trade Magazine Ads	($)	36000	36000	36000	108000
Sales Reps:					
Assigned	($)	18000	18000	18000	54000
Hired	($)	0	0	0	0
Commissions paid	($)	7632	3504	9504	20640
SubTotal	($)	164132	160004	166004	490140
Sales Reps Available	(#)	3	3	3	

Sales & Administration Summary

SELLING		Product 1	Product 2	Total
Product Features Spending	($)	0	0	0
Process Improvement Spending	($)	0	0	0
Web Spending	($)	4000	4000	8000
Newspaper Ads	($)	157500	189000	346500
Consumer Magazine Ads	($)	150000	180000	330000
Trade Magazine Ads	($)	108000	126000	234000
Sales Reps	($)	54000	90000	144000
Commissions Paid	($)	20640	35700	56340
Subtotal	($)	494140	624700	1114840
ADMINISTRATIVE				
Office Expense	($)	20199	9801	30000
Marketing Research	($)	2000	2000	4000
Fines	($)	0	0	0
Refunds	($)	0	0	0
TOTAL S & A EXPENSES		516339	636501	1152840
Product Features	(Total #)	0	0	

Income Statement

	Product 1	Product 2	Total
Sales:			
Territory 1	604200	517500	1121700
Territory 2	277400	255300	532700
Territory 3	752400	400200	1152600
Total Sales	1634000	1173000	2807000
Cost of Goods Sold	946000	459000	1405000
Gross Profit	688000	714000	1402000
S & A	516339	636501	1152840
Inventory Carrying Costs	0	0	0
Operating Profit	171661	77499	249160
Net Interest	0	0	0
Profit Before Taxes	171661	77499	249160
Income Taxes Payable			124580
Net Income			124580

Balance Sheet

ASSETS		LIABILITIES AND OWNERS EQUITY	
Cash	64960	Short-Term Loans Payable	700000
Accounts Receivable	1684200	Taxes Payable	124580
Finished Goods	0		
		Owners Equity	924580
TOTAL ASSETS	1749160	TOTAL LIABILITIES & OWNERS EQUITY	1749160

Cash Flow Statement

CASH RECEIPTS:

Cash On Hand	800000
Collection of A/R	1122800
TOTAL CASH RECEIPTS	1922800

CASH PAYMENTS:

Product Cost Expense	1405000
S & A Expense	1152840
Inventory Carrying Cost	0
Short-Term Interest	0
Short-Term Loan Payment	0
Income Taxes Paid	0
TOTAL CASH PAYMENTS	2557840
NET CASH FLOW	-635040
ST LOAN GRANTED	700000
NET CASH BALANCE	64960

Cost Parameters

GENERAL COSTS

News Ads ($ per 1/8 page)	2500
Consumer Mag Ads (per 1/4 page)	4000
Trade Mag Ads (per 1/2 page)	2000
Sales Reps Salary ($/quarter)	5000
Sales Reps Hire/Train ($/quarter)	8000
Product Base Cost P1	11.00
Product Base Cost P2	27.00
Inventory Carrying Cost P1	1.20
Inventory Carrying Cost P2	2.20
Administrative Expense	30000
Features P1 Mfg ($ / unit)	0.10
Features P2 Mfg ($ / unit)	0.30
Short-Term Loan Rate (%)	10.0

MARKET RESEARCH COSTS

	Per Company	All Companies
Units sold	200	2000
Price	250	2000
Features	750	6000
Quality	750	6000
Web Spending	750	6000
News Ads	250	2000
Consumer Mag Ads	250	2000
Trade Magazine Ads	250	2000
Sales Reps	250	2000
Ad Message	400	4000
Demand Estimates		2000

APPENDIX C

AN EXAMPLE OF AN INDUSTRY PERFORMANCE REPORT

Quarter Peformance Report

COMP	SALES	PTS AWRD	INCOME	PTS AWRD	ROS	PTS AWRD	FORECAST ERRORS	PTS AWRD	OVERALL PTS	RANK
1	3202497	20	137798	25	4.3	17	19163	6	68	7
2	3557057	22	208466	38	5.9	24	21250	5	89	2
3	3154626	19	34331	6	1.1	4	13272	9	39	12
4	3399500	21	219104	40*	6.4	26*	37923	3	90	1
5	3696002	23	75817	14	2.1	8	11664	10*	55	10
6	3539334	22	201136	37	5.7	23	29362	4	85	3
7	3744167	23	115564	21	3.1	12	48929	2	59	9
8	3130817	19	164515	30	5.3	21	28388	4	75	6
9	3887131	24*	118771	22	3.1	12	25921	4	63	8
10	3401613	21	188212	34	5.5	22	23615	5	83	5
11	3417700	21	66717	12	2.0	8	36744	3	44	11
12	3295408	20	187607	34	5.7	23	17113	7	84	4
Ave	3452154		143170		4		26112			

Game To Date Peformance Report

COMP	SALES	PTS AWRD	INCOME	PTS AWRD	ROS	PTS AWRD	FORECAST ERRORS	PTS AWRD	OVERALL PTS	RANK
1	9047022	21	478968	32	5.3	21	31546	7	81	7
2	9509041	22	563589	38	5.9	24	28723	8	91	3
3	9196079	21	296601	20	3.2	13	38909	6	59	12
4	9235631	21	595722	40*	6.5	26*	50216	4	91	2
5	10166450	23	355871	24	3.5	14	49804	4	65	10
6	9518011	22	553594	37	5.8	23	43954	5	87	4
7	10246630	23	443964	30	4.3	17	116636	2	72	8
8	8889078	20	532487	36	6.0	24	40890	5	85	6
9	10539430	24*	426316	29	4.0	16	75942	3	72	9
10	9238760	21	518286	35	5.6	23	25932	8	87	5
11	9622161	22	358642	24	3.7	15	95714	2	63	11
12	9177432	21	559955	38	6.1	25	21600	10*	93	1
Ave	9532143		473666		5		51656			

APPENDIX D

AN EXAMPLE OF A MARKETING RESEARCH REPORT

							Cons.	Trade	Sales	Ad
Co. #	Units Sold	Price	Features	Quality	Web	News	Mags	Mags	Reps	Msg
1	4648	37.00	0	0.00	8000	15	10	12	3	Service
2	33013	20.11	3	0.60	14347	11	11	10	5	Quality
3	39177	18.41	0	0.14	28789	17	8	9	3	Price
4	31399	19.35	1	0.56	6000	9	3	6	5	Service
5	38700	18.71	0	0.27	17123	18	12	13	4	Features
6	30237	19.49	1	0.57	13385	8	6	8	5	Quality
7	37317	18.73	0	0.16	25000	12	9	9	3	Price
8	31695	19.38	1	0.56	6000	10	3	6	5	Service
9	43342	18.57	1	0.28	24751	19	12	15	4	Features
10	31840	19.65	2	0.55	14636	14	10	7	4	Quality
11	46339	18.44	0	0.17	29012	18	12	13	3	Price
12	29487	19.35	1	0.64	6000	6	3	7	6	Service

Marketing Research - Product 1

Territory 1

Demand Estimate for Quarter   4   414000   Demand Estimate for Quarter   5   386400

Territory 1   Territory 2   Territory 3

The demand estimates you see here (414000 and 386400) represent the *total combined demand* (in units) for all companies in the industry for Territory 1.

Demand for Quarter 1.

Because you cannot purchase demand estimates for Quarter 1, we supply them here.

Unless your simulation administrator informs you otherwise, the demand estimates for Quarter 1 are:

Product 1

Territory 1	Territory 2	Territory 3
31800	14600	39600

Product 2

Territory 1	Territory 2	Territory 3
7500	3700	5800

These demand estimates for Quarter 1 represent the *average number* of units that will be sold by a *single company* in your industry. Thus, the 31,800 figure is an estimate of the number of units of Product 1 that an *average firm* will sell in Territory 1 in the first Quarter. **In all future periods, the demand estimates represent the *total number* of units that will be sold in your entire industry.** The 414000 figure shown on the Marketing Research Report is an estimate of *total industry demand*.

APPENDIX E
INITIAL COST PARAMETERS

Cost Parameters	☒

GENERAL COSTS		MARKET RESEARCH COSTS		
			Per Company	All Companies
News Ads ($ per 1/8 page)	2500			
Consumer Mag Ads (per 1/4 page)	4000	Units sold	200	2000
Trade Mag Ads (per 1/2 page)	2000	Price	250	2000
Sales Reps Salary ($/quarter)	5000	Features	750	6000
Sales Reps Hire/Train ($/quarter)	8000	Quality	750	6000
Product Base Cost P1	11.00	Web Spending	750	6000
Product Base Cost P2	27.00	News Ads	250	2000
Inventory Carrying Cost P1	1.20	Consumer Mag Ads	250	2000
Inventory Carrying Cost P2	2.20	Trade Magazine Ads	250	2000
Administrative Expense	30000	Sales Reps	250	2000
Features P1 Mfg ($ / unit)	0.10	Ad Message	400	4000
Features P2 Mfg ($ / unit)	0.30			
Short-Term Loan Rate (%)	10.0	Demand Estimates		2000

APPENDIX F

THE TIMING OF YOUR ACTIONS

Decisions Made **This** Quarter	Impact On **This** Quarter (e.g., Qtr 1)	Impact On **Following** Quarter (e.g., Qtr 2)
Set price	Affects sales	Change in price affects sales
Newspaper ad ordered	Affects expenditures and sales	No carryover effects.
Consumer magazine. ad ordered	Affects expenditures and sales	Has some carryover effect on sales
Trade magazine. ad ordered	Affects expenditures and sales	Has some carryover effect on sales
Ad message chosen	Message is used; affects sales	No carryover effects.
Salesperson hired	Individual is in training Affects expenditures Doesn't affect sales	Individual is on staff, Affects sales and expenditures
Salesperson fired	Salesperson is gone Affects expenditures	No carryover effects.
Salespersons on staff	Affects sales and expenditures	No carryover effects.
Commission	Affects sales and expenditures	No carryover effects.
Product quality	Affects sales and expenditures	Some carryover effect on sales.
Web spending	Affects sales and expenditures	No carryover effects.
Product ordered	No effect this quarter.	Affects expenditures; Product is received
Product features	Affects expenditures	Affects sales, if feature is added
Process improvement	Affects expenditures	Affects product cost
ST loan request	Loan is received	Interest charges on loan due.
Marketing research ordered	Affects expenditures	Research purchased is received

DECISION LIMITS:

The Price Limits Differ for the Two Products
Maximum prices: Product 1 = $49.99; Product 2 = $149.99

All of the Following Limits are the Same for Product 1 and for Product 2
Quality: $99.99/ unit
Maximum number of Ads (per territory):
    Newspaper Ads   99
    Consumer Magazine Ads   99
    Trade Magazine Ads   99
Maximum number of Sales Rep hires and fires (per territory)   99
Maximum Commission: 99%
Web Spending $99,999
Sales Forecast (per territory)   99,999 units
Product Ordered (per territory)   99,999 units
Product Features Development $99,999
Process Improvement $99,999
Short-Term Loan $3,000,000

APPENDIX G
MERLIN "HOT" KEYS

<u>Screen</u>	<u>"Hot" Key(s)</u>
To see	**Press**

Decisions

Decisions Report – Product 1	F1
Decisions Report – Product 1	F2
Marketing Research Decisions Report – Product 1	F3
Marketing Research Decisions Report – Product 2	F4

Reports

Decisions Report – Product 1	Shift + F1
Decisions Report – Product 2	Shift + F2
Marketing Research Decisions – Product 1	Shift + F3
Marketing Research Decisions – Product 2	Shift + F4
Production Costs	CTRL + P
Inventory	CTRL + V
Product 1 Report	
Product 2 Report	
Selling/Administration	CTRL + S
Income Statement	CTRL + I
Balance Sheet	CTRL + B
Cash Flow	CTRL + C
Marketing Research Report – Product 1	
Marketing Research Report – Product 2	
Quarter Performance	CTRL + Q
Game-to-Date Performance	CTRL + G

Info

Marketing Limits	
Production Limits	
Costs	F5
Bulletin	F6

APPENDIX H
Excel Company Data File

Excel Column	Variable Name	Definition
A	Quarter	
B	P1PrT1	Product 1, Price, Territory 1
C	P1Feat	Product 1, # of features
D	P1Qual	Product 1, $ amount spent on quality
E	P1PrSav	Product 1, $ amount of process savings
F	WebSp	$ amount of web spending
G	P1NwsT1	Product 1, # of newspaper ads, Territory 1
H	P1CMT1	Product 1, # of consumer magazine ads, Territory 1
I	P1TMT1	Product 1, # of trade magazine ads, Territory 1
J	P1MsgT1	Product 1, Advertising message, Territory 1 (0=Price; 1= Features; 2=Quality; 3= Service; 4=Benefits)
K	P1SFT1	Product 1, # of sales reps, Territory 1
L	P1ComT1	Product 1, Salesforce commission, Territory 1
M	P1UnitT1	Product 1, Unit sales, Territory 1
N	P1InvT1	Product 1, Ending inventory, Territory 1
O	P1PrT2	Product 1, Price, Territory 2
P	P1NwsT2	Product 1, # of newspaper ads, Territory 2
Q	P1CMT2	Product 1, # of consumer magazine ads, Territory 2
R	P1TMT2	Product 1, # of trade magazine ads, Territory 2
S	P1MsgT2	Product 1, Advertising message, Territory 2 (0=Price; 1= Features; 2=Quality; 3= Service; 4=Benefits)
T	P1SFT2	Product 1, # of sales reps, Territory 2
U	P1ComT2	Product 1, Salesforce commission, Territory 2
V	P1UnitT2	Product 1, Unit sales, Territory 2
W	P1InvT2	Product 1, Ending inventory, Territory 2
X	P1PrT3	Product 1, Price, Territory 3
Y	P1NwsT3	Product 1, # of newspaper ads, Territory 3
Z	P1CMT3	Product 1, # of consumer magazine ads, Territory 3
AA	P1TMT3	Product 1, # of trade magazine ads, Territory 3
AB	P1MsgT3	Product 1, Advertising message, Territory 3 (0=Price; 1= Features; 2=Quality; 3= Service; 4=Benefits)
AC	P1SFT3	Product 1, # of sales reps, Territory 3
AD	P1ComT3	Product 1, Salesforce commission, Territory 3
AE	P1UnitT3	Product 1, Unit sales, Territory 3
AF	P1InvT3	Product 1, Ending inventory, Territory 3
AG	P2PrT1	Product 2, Price, Territory 1
AH	P2Feat	Product 2, # of features
AI	P2Qual	Product 2, $ amount spent on quality

AJ	P2PrSav	Product 1, $ amount of process savings
AK	P2NewsT1	Product 2, # of newspaper ads, Territory 1
AL	P2CMT1	Product 2, # of consumer magazine ads, Territory 1
AM	P2TMT1	Product 2, # of trade magazine ads, Territory 1
AN	P2MsgT1	Product 2, Advertising message, Territory 1 (0=Price; 1= Features; 2=Quality; 3= Service; 4=Benefits)
AO	P2SFT1	Product 2, # of sales reps, Territory 1
AP	P2ComT1	Product 2, Salesforce commission, Territory 1
AQ	P2UnitT1	Product 2, Unit sales, Territory 1
AR	P2InvT1	Product 2, Ending inventory, Territory 1
AS	P2PrT2	Product 2, Price, Territory 2
AT	P2NewsT2	Product 2, # of newspaper ads, Territory 2
AU	P2CMT2	Product 2, # of consumer magazine ads, Territory 2
AV	P2TMT2	Product 2, # of trade magazine ads, Territory 2
AW	P2MsgT2	Product 2, Advertising message, Territory 2 (0=Price; 1= Features; 2=Quality; 3= Service; 4=Benefits)
AX	P2SFT2	Product 2, # of sales reps, Territory 2
AY	P2ComT2	Product 2, Salesforce commission, Territory 2
AZ	P2UnitT2	Product 2, Unit sales, Territory 2
BA	P2InvT2	Product 2, Ending inventory, Territory 2
BB	P2PrT3	Product 2, Price, Territory 3
BC	P2NewsT3	Product 2, # of newspaper ads, Territory 3
BD	P2CMT3	Product 2, # of consumer magazine ads, Territory 3
BE	P2TMT3	Product 2, # of trade magazine ads, Territory 3
BF	P2MsgT3	Product 2, Advertising message, Territory 3 (0=Price; 1= Features; 2=Quality; 3= Service; 4=Benefits)
BG	P2SFT3	Product 2, # of sales reps, Territory 3
BH	P2ComT3	Product 2, Salesforce commission, Territory 3
BI	P2UnitT3	Product 2, Unit sales, Territory 3
BJ	P2InvT3	Product 2, Ending inventory, Territory 3

APPENDIX I
Excel Performance Data File

Excel Column	Variable Name	Definition
A	Quarter	
B	Company	Company number
C	QSales$	Quarterly sales in $
D	QtrInc	Quarterly income
E	QROS	Quarterly return on sales
F	Qrank	Quarterly rank
G	CumSales	Cumulative sales
H	CumInc	Cumulative income
I	CumROS	Cumulative return on sales
J	CumRank	Cumulative rank

APPENDIX J
MERLIN FLOW CHART

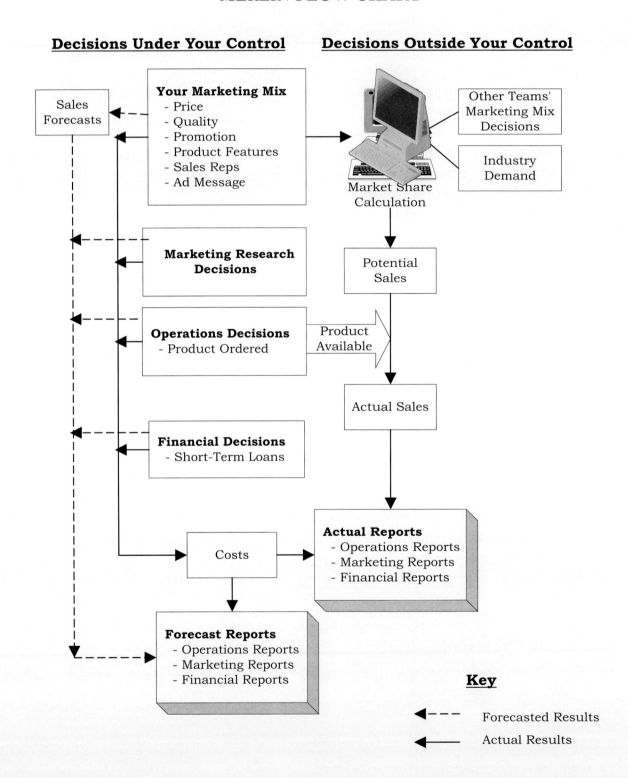

Decisions Under Your Control

Decisions Outside Your Control

Sales Forecasts

Your Marketing Mix
- Price
- Quality
- Promotion
- Product Features
- Sales Reps
- Ad Message

Market Share Calculation

Other Teams' Marketing Mix Decisions

Industry Demand

Marketing Research Decisions

Potential Sales

Operations Decisions
- Product Ordered

Product Available

Financial Decisions
- Short-Term Loans

Actual Sales

Costs

Actual Reports
- Operations Reports
- Marketing Reports
- Financial Reports

Forecast Reports
- Operations Reports
- Marketing Reports
- Financial Reports

Key

Forecasted Results

Actual Results

APPENDIX K
A STEP-BY-STEP WALK-THROUGH

The purpose of this "walk-through" exercise is to familiarize you with navigating and working with Merlin. Completing this exercise will help you understand and feel comfortable working with the program.

1. Start the *Merlin Solo* program.

2. Press the F2 "hot" key key to move to the Product 2 Decisions screen.

3. Enter some decisions for Product 2.
   - Raise price of Product 2 by $1.35.
   - Buy 15 Trade magazine ads for Product 2.
   - Lower sales forecast for Product 2 by 1,500 units.

4. Press the F4 "hot" key key to move to the Marketing Research Decisions screen for Product 2.
   - Buy Price and Units Sold information for all three territories for companies 5 and 9.
   - Buy Demand Estimates for Product 2 for Quarters 2 and 3.

5. Look at the Forecast reports.
   - Use mouse to select the Reports option on the Menu bar
   - Select a report; e.g., the Income Statement.

6. Press the F5 "hot" key to access the Cost screen.
   - Notice the cost of Trade magazine ads is $2,000 (listed in the left column, third item).

7. Press the F2 "hot" key to return to the Product 2 Decisions.

8. Vary your decisions.
   - Lower the Trade magazine ads for Product 2 by 5.
   - Lower the sales forecast for Product 2 by another 600 units to reflect the decrease in promotion effort.

9. Look at the Income Statement again (use the Ctrl + I "hot" keys to go directly to the Income Statement).
   - Notice the change in the Net Income from first forecast.

10. Process the Decisions.
    - Select the File option on the Menu bar.
    - Select the Process Industry option.
    - Notice how the quarter number in the Menu bar has changed from 1 to 2.

11. Look at the Actual reports.
    - Select the Quarter option on the Menu bar.
    - Choose the "1". Notice the how the Menu bar now says Quarter 1 and <u>Actuals</u> rather than <u>Forecast</u>.
    - Look at the Inventory report under the Reports option on the Menu bar.
      - Notice Units Sold line for Product 2 and any difference from the Sales Forecast you entered earlier.
    - Look at the Income Statement (See Point #9)
      - Notice the change in Net Income from what was forecast.

12. Print out selected reports.
    - Select the Print option on the Menu bar.
    - Choose the Selected Screens option.
    - Click on the Income Statement and the Cash Flow options, then click on OK.
    - Click OK when the Printer dialogue box appears.

13. Restart at Quarter 1 (or repeat Steps 2 through 9 for Quarter 2, to continue to Quarter 3).
    - Select the File option on the Menu bar.
    - Choose the Start New Game option.
    - Notice how the Menu bar shows that you are back to the Quarter 1 Forecast.

14. Exit *Merlin Solo.*
    - Select the File option on the Menu bar and then Exit.

INDEX